THE WHO

Daltrey as Tommy, on stage at the New York Metropolitan Opera House, 1969.

GARY HERMAN

STUDIO VISTA

Produced by November Books Limited, 23–29 Emerald Street, London, WC1N 3QL.

Published by Studio Vista Limited, Blue Star House, Highgate Hill, London, N19.

Text set by Trade Linotype Limited, Birmingham 7.

Printed by Compton Printing Limited, Pembroke Road, Stocklake, Aylesbury, Bucks.

Bound by Dorstel Press Limited, West Road, Templefields, Harlow, Essex.

© *November Books Limited 1971.*

Printed in England.

This edition is not for sale in the United States of America.

Dust-jacket and paperback cover designed by David Goard.

Designed by Tom Carter.
House editor: Tony Russell.
Copy preparation: John Leath.

SBN 289.70135.x (hardback)
289.70134.1 (paperback)

Series edited by Phil Hardy

ACKNOWLEDGEMENTS

I thank all the many friends who helped me with ideas and in more concrete ways, including Mal, John and Alan.

I am indebted to Dave Ruffel of Track Records, without whom this book could never have been begun, let alone finished. I am also very grateful to Vernon Brewer and everyone else at Track, and to my editor, Phil Hardy.

The lyrics of all The Who's compositions are quoted by kind permission of Fabulous Music, Ltd., and New Ikon, Ltd. The quotation from Going Back *(Goffin-King, 1966) is used by kind permission of Screen Gems-Columbia Music, Ltd.*

Photographs reproduced by kind permission of Track Records. (Special credits: John Entwhistle 102, 103, 105; Essex Music 83; Fair Enterprises 46; Graham Hughes 28b, 100; Eric Jelly 64; Chris Morphet 16; Lee Morphet 11.)

CONTENTS

Talking 'bout my generation	7
The noonday underground	19
Maximum R & B	29
Extraordinary sensations	39
Songs of innocence, songs of experience	59
See me, feel me, touch me	71
I can see for miles	81
Notes	94

Appendix
   Interviews with Roger Daltrey and
      John Entwhistle
	95

Discography	108

Releasing pent-up aggression: Moon and collapsing drum kit, Monterey Pop Festival, 1968.

Talking 'bout My Generation

> Need a shot of rhythm and blues,
> With just a little rock 'n' roll on the side,
> Just for good measure.
>
> Johnny Kidd, 1962

On a rainy night in late 1964, a group called The Who made their first appearance at the Marquee Club, Wardour Street, in the West End of London. Keith Moon literally attacked his drums, breaking several drumsticks in the process and ending the performance with his clothes stuck to him and his jaw sagging from exhaustion. Roger Daltrey, shouting until he was hoarse, dripping with sweat, smashed his microphone into the floor. Pete Townshend, known as 'The Birdman' because of the way he spun his arms in the air like propellors, rammed the neck of his guitar into its amplifier until the guitar split in two. John Entwhistle, the bass guitarist, stood a discreet distance apart, dressed in black, quite still. Although the Marquee was one of the best and most popular mod clubs in London (and therefore Britain) and elaborate precautions had been taken beforehand by The Who's co-managers, Chris Stamp and Kit Lambert, there were less than two hundred people there.

Lambert and Stamp chose the Marquee for the group's first appearance in the West End because they were aiming at a mod audience. They approached Ziggy Jackson, mod impresario and populariser of the mod trend of a few months earlier, Blue Beat, a derivative of a West Indian dance rhythm known as Ska. They pressured him for weeks. Finally, he agreed that The Who should do a trial run at the Marquee on Tuesday nights (the worst night of the week for audiences). Lambert and Stamp were to promote the show themselves.

Since their 'primary concern was to get an audience', as Lambert explained, they invested most of their money and effort in advertisement; their costs came to £300. They printed 1,500 posters for the whole of London and 2,500 handouts to be given away at dances, clubs, coffee bars, markets and so on. They emphasised the group's

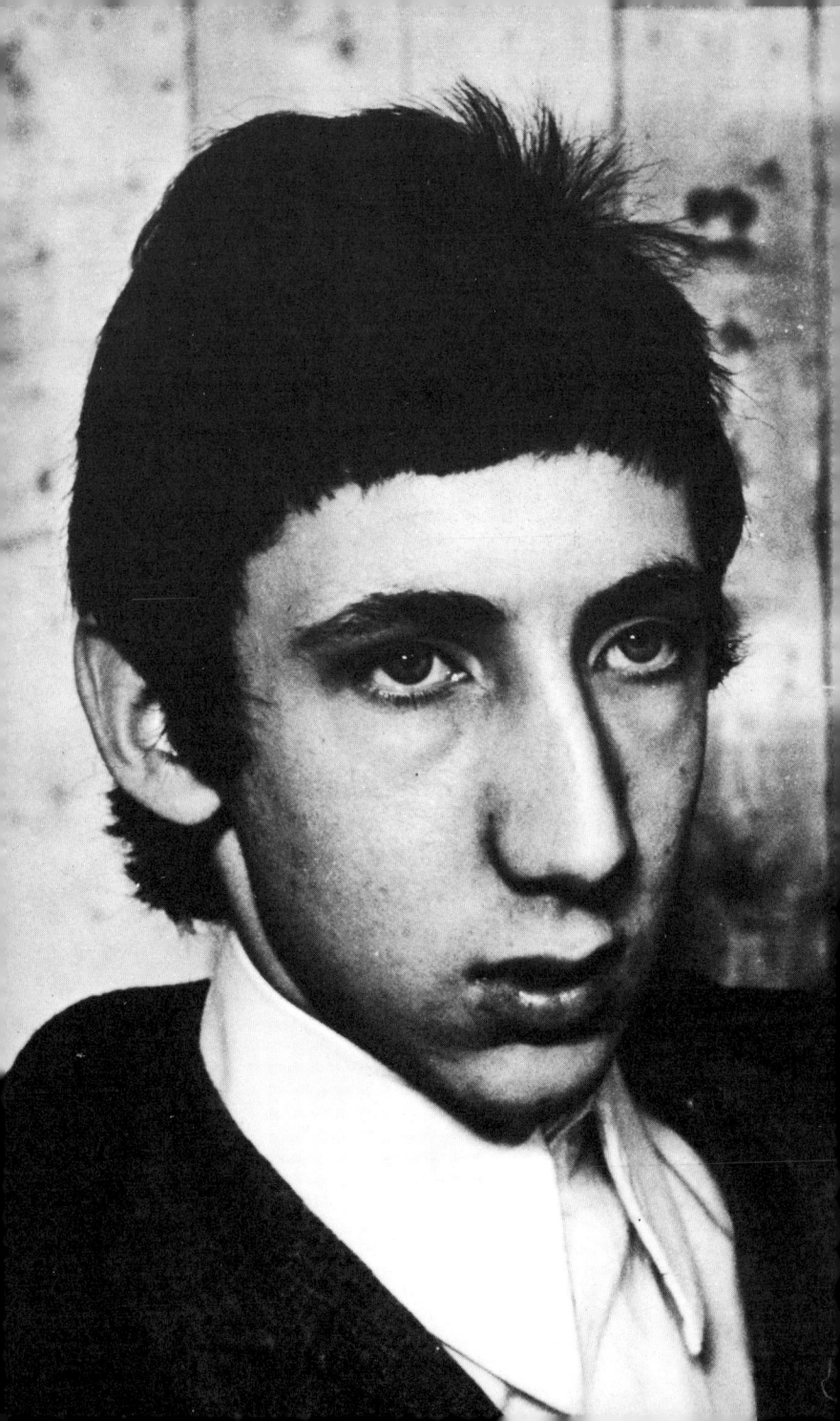

home area, Shepherd's Bush. Like every band from The Beatles on, The Who needed a clear geographical location, as with 'The Mersey Sound' before and 'The San Francisco Sound' after. This was to be 'The Shepherd's Bush Sound'.

Every street in the area was covered; thirty of the local mods were given free tickets, and yet more tickets were sold at half-price to members of a mod club which Lambert and Stamp had formed for the occasion, The 100 Faces. Some time later, in 1966, The Who's managers explained why they went to all that trouble: 'We realised that if the group were to build up any national following, we must take the West End.' For months before, Lambert and Stamp had been promoting the group with no luck at all. They often worked 17 hours a day, following their regular jobs as assistant film directors and afterwards chasing record pluggers, disc jockeys and music companies, entertaining important people, spending savings of hundreds of pounds – all fruitlessly.

The record boom was over. It was to be expected that, following the incredible explosion of 'Beatlemania' in 1963 and early 1964, things would seem comparatively mild by late 1964. Moreover, the rise of The Beatles did not signify any drastic change in the nature or structure of the record industry; such change was only to come later, when people realised that the Beatle period had not heralded a permanent boom, and that the industry needed to realign itself to sustain the economically buoyant position The Beatles had created. Nor was their sound very different or new. A mixture of The Everly Brothers, The Miracles and Little Richard but with a Liverpool accent, its major virtue was that it had a refreshing crudeness and provinciality after the commercialised, synthetic slickness of the American-dominated pre-1963 record scene. The kids who reached puberty at the beginning of the '60s could relate to the music of ex-members of neighbourhood gangs in Liverpool more than they ever could to the factory products of Neil Sedaka, Bobby Vee and countless other American and English 'All-American' boys and girls.

That is not to say that no good music was produced between 1959 and 1963. There was still some life left in rock 'n' roll. However, the peak years were over by 1960. Haley had failed to progress after *Rock Around The Clock* (a number recorded several years before it became popular); Presley was in the army and later turned to singing ballads; Little Richard had become a gospel singer; Eddie Cochran was killed and Gene Vincent injured in the same car crash. Even so, 1959 to 1962 saw the best years of an English rock 'n' roller, Johnny Kidd, who ran a close second to Eddie Cochran, before he too died in a road accident. (Kidd's biggest hit, *Shakin' All Over*, made in 1960, is featured on The Who's 'Live At Leeds' album, and in a BBC broadcast before the release of the album, Pete Townshend cited Kidd as a formative influence.) On the whole, however, the spontaneous vitality of rock 'n' roll had been sapped by the eager rush to cash in on this new music of the new young. It would, nevertheless, be an exaggeration to claim that the rest of the music produced between 1959 and 1963 was mediocre. Much of it was of a quality

Townshend on stage in boiler suit, New York Metropolitan Opera House, 1970.

that English rock took years to surpass. Sedaka, The Everlys, the Tamla-Motown groups and Phil Spector's all-girl groups made records which revealed a familiarity with the electronic medium about four years in advance of anything English recording studios could display. One has the feeling that Phil Spector knew all about multi-tracking before most English producers knew what it was.

The only disadvantage of this sophistication was its sterility. It represented the institutionalisation of what was essentially a vital musical form – rock 'n' roll. It was as though Chuck Berry's *Sweet Little Sixteen* had been re-recorded as Neil Sedaka's *Happy Birthday Sweet Sixteen* and, in the process of gaining a super-professional veneer, had lost all the original vitality and feeling. On the other hand, The Who's use of electronic sound-effects and mixing reveals in their music the perfect synthesis of The Beatles' crudity and American electronic sophistication. The Who's electronics, both on stage and in the studio, do not merely dress up their songs but enhance them. Occasionally, as in *I'm A Man* from the 'My Generation' album, their technique is seen to be far superior to their feeling for other people's songs. Yet *Summertime Blues* and *Shakin' All Over* are enormously improved by advanced electronic instrumentation. Cochran's and Kidd's songs, lyrically and melodically fragmented, gain considerable power from the 'continuous wall of sound' which electronic instrumentation can now provide. It acts as a back-cloth against which the fragmentary nature of the songs (both actual and symbolic) is highlighted.

What was lacking in the music of the early '60s, what distinguished it from the technically just as sophisticated music of The Who, was the special relationship that rock 'n' roll music and musicians had with the people who listened and danced to rock 'n' roll. This special relationship was central to rock 'n' roll and to the rock music that developed out of it. In many ways it can be seen as the primary difference between rock and pop; certainly it separates rock 'n' roll from the early '60s pop music which masqueraded as rock 'n' roll.

Rock music is undeniably a form of popular music, both historically, in terms of the natural development of rock, and socially, in terms of the number and kinds of people who listen to and often participate in some form of rock. The distinction between rock and pop music corresponds to the crude physical distinction between younger and older generations. Historically speaking, therefore, the 'Age of Rock' began in 1956 with the release of Haley's *Rock Around The Clock*. But the distinction is far larger than that. To encapsulate it in two overworked words: rock is progressive, pop reactionary.

All popular music revolutions – that is, all large-scale shifts in taste and style – are the direct result of analogous shifts in the tastes and styles of the people who listen to and participate in that music. Now these shifts occur at a level where distinctions between audience and performer are mutually agreed upon. The idea of the performer as a separate individual, removed from the social group to which he per-

'Dedicated Follower of Fashion' – 1: *Daltrey on stage, 1966.*

forms and surrounded by all the symbols of material success and economic superiority, is one that only occurs with the commercial exploitation of the music. The Merseyside of the late '50s and early '60s which Colin Fletcher describes in 'Beat and Gangs on Merseyside'[1] provides a case in point. The groups that formed in the area in the late '50s were such that they provided a locus of activity for the gangs and the gangs were the source of both group members and audiences. 'The group', as Fletcher puts it, 'became the gang's totem.' Strictly speaking the relationship between gang and group cannot be defined as totemic, yet there are structural similarities between each clan within a tribe and each gang within a socio-geographic group, and consequently between totem and rock-group. The fact that the individuals who form the rock-group are also members of the gang implies that the relationship is more complex and only totemic on one level. Many rock-groups took zoological names (The Beatles), or names with a significance in an identifiable mythology (The Rolling Stones), and this indicates the degree to which they could accurately be described as totems. In this context, the music was a participatory phenomenon on every level, and gang and group entered into a symbiotic relationship. The gang provided performers, financial aid, support of every kind, often even the uniforms the group wore. In return, the group was the primary source of the music which was the gang's chief interest. More than that, the group and its music provided a bond that was eventually to overcome the exclusiveness and territorial restrictions of individual gangs. Several gangs would meet under one roof to listen and dance to the music of several groups; the groups extended the bounds of what Fletcher calls 'neutral territory'. In this way, the neighbourhood groups and their music provided The focus of a collective awareness and the locus of a collective experience, features which are characteristic of rock to a degree unknown in any earlier form of white popular music. Initially the groups were instrumental both in creating a collective consciousness, a subculture outside traditional culture, and in expressing it. We shall see later how that role was exploited by commercial interests, how 'restriction by partial incorporation' effectively transformed the symbiotic relationship into the alienated form that exists inside the rock music industry. This process, in which the massive popularisation of rock's innovations almost always involves attempts to standardise those innovations within an existing commercial framework, is familiar throughout the history of rock, if not of popular music in general. The history of the 'Mersey Beat' not only provides a well-documented archetype, but is also directly relevant to the development of The Who and to the context in which their music achieved popularity.

The shift in taste and style that created the Mersey Beat phenomenon was essentially the same as all other shifts in popular music. An already operational form – in the case of Mersey Beat it was rock 'n' roll and the pop music of the late '50s – is taken over by what is initially a minority group and transformed by the peculiar circumstances of the group's nature. Parochial or ethnic interpretations are made, both of style and of content, and, what is perhaps more impor-

Entwhistle 'dressed all in black' at The Roundhouse. London, 1969.

tant, circumstances often cause the music to develop totally different formal structures and organisations. For example, the ease with which electric guitars could be purchased on credit in Britain in the early '60s allowed bands to play the kind of music that had previously been recorded with a line-up of saxophones, pianos and so forth. This now became guitar music; the same quantity of noise was available, but it was cheaper and easier to obtain. That alone was not the cause of any particular change, but it gave a tremendous impetus to the shift away from orchestrated big-band music, towards a more anarchic

Chris Stamp and Kit Lambert outside Caroline House, 1965, when pirate radio was big and The Who weren't.

electric music ideally suited to small guitar-based bands. Similar effects can be seen in the development of blues, jazz and latter-day rock, in all of which changes have occurred at least partly in response to the 'borrowing' of techniques and styles that have become readily obtainable. Thus the blues, for example, has been shaped by the adaptation of white styles and techniques to black modes of expression and the transformation of both these elements in the light of the unique circumstances of the black American.

Such changes in popular music, which are fundamental because they involve changes in the conception of the music, tend to be initiated by the convergence of two or more cultural modes, aided, as often as not, by economic necessities. It is worth noting the important role played by ports or towns built at the junction of large communications product by using different numerical series. Although the record industry's use of the word 'race' was still widespread in 1950 the major companies had formed subsidiary labels with which black music could be identified. RCA Victor used Bluebird and Columbia had OKeh. Asch's field recordings appeared on many different labels, including Varsity and Columbia, but others were not made available until the latter half of the century, when they appeared in collections aimed primarily at white folk-blues enthusiasts.

Like the majority of gospel records made prior to 1950, the Thrasher family's recording of *Moses Smote The Water* was performed *a capella*. Negro churches in the South were inevitably humble buildings made from clapboard and corrugated iron without any ornate decoration. What had become of the reed 'quills', cigar-box guitars and cornstalk fiddles is not certain. Perhaps the rhythm produced on these and other home-made instruments of slavery was inappropriate, for they are not in evidence on the earliest gospel recordings. In any event, the rural church could seldom afford instruments and rhythm was provided by the voices of the performers and the hands and feet of the congregation, encouraged by their preacher's reference to Psalm 47 – 'Oh clap your hands, all ye people, shout unto the Lord with the voice of triumph'. If they prospered, instruments were still limited. Unlike black jazz musicians in the big cities, the isolated country negro had no access to exotic percussion or woodwind and he was left to embellish his music with a rudimentary tambourine or, if fortunate, a piano. In consequence, drums were not introduced to gospel recordings until they were used by Roberta Martin on Savoy as late as 1950. Their arrival helped compensate for the lack of an audience at recording sessions.

The bass vocal on thirty Drifters records is taken by Bill Pinkney, who first met Gerhart Thrasher when he left his brothers and sisters to join a more successful group, The Jerusalem Stars. Pinkney, born on 15 August 1925 in Sumpter, South Carolina, had been singing bass with other childhood gospel units ever since his voice had broken. With The Singing Cousins (Mathew Gallashaw, Herb and David Glover and Wesley and James Mack) and The Wandering Four he had been out on the road amongst the small townships of the Alabama and Carolina backwoods. With The Jerusalem Stars, who also included Bill Massey, Jimmy Griffin and Brook Benton, Thrasher and Pinkney toured much of the South, preferring church halls to dilapidated theatres or storefront wooden shacks. They wrote and arranged their own material and occasionally appeared with famous names like Brother Cleophus Robinson in a gospel-rama held to commemorate a special occasion; perhaps New Year's Eve, or a well-known group's celebration of its fifth anniversary. Today similar concerts take place almost every week in the major cities of the United States, but the instrumentation now includes a guitar and organ, and a vocal 'battle' between two of the more dynamic groups is usually a highlight. It would serve little purpose to list the credentials of other gospel-singing Drifters; suffice it to say that of those interviewed only one member, Bobby Hendricks, failed to disclose an upbringing strongly connected with the church.

It is a fact that much of today's gospel tends to be reheated versions of old R&B tunes, but during the '50s and early '60s, R&B stole gospel tunes and their arrangements. Hank Ballard's *What Is This I See* (King 5491) came from The Sensational Nightingales' incredibly morbid *Standing At The Judgement* (Peacock 1804); Ray Charles' *I Got A Woman* (Atlantic 1050) was a secularisation of *My Jesus Is All The World To Me*; and Theola Kilgore's *The Love Of My Man* (Serock 2004) was merely *The Love Of Jesus* with one or two appropriate alterations. In *Something's Got A Hold On Me* (*It Must Be The Lord*) Etta James altered the words 'The Lord' to 'Love' and reached the Top Twenty with the result (Argo 5409). Ben E King's massive hit *Stand By Me* (Atco 6194) is said to owe a great deal lyrically and musically to Sam Cooke and The Soul Stirrers' recording of *Be With Me, Jesus* (Specialty 878). The Drifters' treatment of many of their earliest recordings similarly borrowed the gospel techniques which I have outlined. The humorous rock 'n' roll number *Money Honey* contained traces of a gospel approach, whilst *The Bells Of St Mary* was soaked in religious sentiment.

White Christmas *was the first Drifters' record to turn from R&B to popular success. From* Cashbox, *1954.*

"WHITE CHRISTMAS" (2:35)
[Berlin ASCAP—Berlin]

"THE BELLS OF ST. MARY" (2:37)
[Chappell ASCAP—Furber, Adams]

THE DRIFTERS
(Atlantic 1048; 45-1048)

THE DRIFTERS

● Very few original rhythm and blues records ever make the grade as pop hits. Roy Hamilton's "You'll Never Walk Alone" was about the last to do this. But now another one is on the horizon. It's a fabulous recording of the favorite "White Christmas" by the Drifters. The group is one of the best in the R & B field and features the thrilling tenor voice of Clyde McPhatter. The tune has about a million recordings to date, but the way Clyde and the boys render it, it becomes a new and exciting song. Bill Pinckney is the bass voice. Side really jumps. Flip is a bluesy version of "Bells Of St. Mary." "White Christmas" is already hitting in the R & B market and shows signs of reaching the top. If the distribs concentrate on it, they could break it pop.

In church, whoever took the solo could use his voice in a number of different ways to achieve the same purpose. A beautifully clear, high pitched tenor would affect the listener by sheer purity of tune and instil greater devotion to God. (Equally beautiful voices are found in Welsh choral singing and are probably intended to have a similar effect.) But there was also a highly emotional approach. Paul Arnold, lead with The Gospelaires, has one of the most terrifying voices in the whole of modern gospel, second only to that of The Reverend Julius Cheeks. It is a raw, slurred, passionate wail – as if the vocal chords were full of spittle. The intensity of his performance involves the audience. Had he crooned the words 'do you believe' instead of hurling them out in a gargled scream, his hearers would have had less reason to be filled with godly worship. McPhatter's fragile tenor was unsuited to the hoarse, unrestrained technique, but he tried both, and demonstrated a less controlled approach on a remarkable recording entitled *The Bells* (Federal 12114) made with The Dominoes in 1950. As he may have done years before in his father's church, he breaks down; the lyric deteriorates into a succession of sobs as he pretends to be overcome by emotion and loses control of his voice.

When gospel singers crossed over the line, their uninhibited and energetic methods of worship were easily transferred to the performance of exuberant rock 'n' roll material. It no longer became necessary to feel the spirit before one moved, and many a performer found that leaping off-stage to excite a theatre audience was no more difficult than running down the aisle amongst the congregation. *The Bells* suggests that, during its performance, McPhatter would have fallen to his knees to emphasise that his lack of control did not affect only his voice. Referring to others like McPhatter, Charles Keil has written:

The climactic feature of a cry singer's act comes at the point where he falls on one knee and asks the audience 'Did you evah cry?' or another question about suffering and soul that can be answered with an affirmative shout. This technique stems directly from earlier experience with spiritual groups.[8]

Try Try Baby, *There You Go*, *Honey Love* and *Such A Night*, all 1953/4 recordings by McPhatter and The Drifters, contain many elements of their fifteen years' experience in gospel singing, but *Whatcha Gonna Do* is not only the finest example of gospel-inspired material they were ever to record, it is also their best up-tempo performance. It was made in New York in November 1953 by McPhatter (lead), Gerhart Thrasher (tenor), Andrew Thrasher (baritone), Bill Pinkney (bass) and the group's resident guitarist, Jimmy Oliver. Written by Atlantic chief Ahmet Ertegun (under the reverse pseudonym of Nugetre), the lyrics are simple but most compelling.

> Now whatcha gonna do
> About half past eight? (×2)
> It would knock me out,
> Yes, if we had a date.
>
> You know you're so pretty (you're so pretty),
> Lawdy, looka there (looka there, looka there),
> Yes, you're so pretty (you're so pretty),
> Lawdy, looka there (looka there, looka there),
> Just struttin' down the street (just struttin down the street),
> Long black wavy hair (black wavy hair).

But for the words, there can scarcely have been any difference between the singers' religious and subsequent secular performances. The atmosphere engendered is one of spontaneous joy – a hysterical pleasure in communication, in simply being alive. McPhatter seems to shout with greater force than at any other time in his career, and Gerhart Thrasher's tenor is somehow rich, passionate and strangely moving despite the speed with which the song is delivered. The Drifters echo McPhatter's vocal refrain; the words he has barely finished singing are repeated in harmony by the rest of the group.

Brought up in the time-honoured tradition of antiphony in innumerable church services, black group singers perfectly naturally adapted it to popular music. Perhaps unconsciously it had a most welcome effect. By emphasising the already repetitive lyric and adding an infectious sing-along quality, the possibility of success with a largely juvenile audience, who looked for an easily remembered phrase or hook-line, was greatly enhanced. Its earliest origins were undoubtedly in African tribal music, but it was embellished over two and a half centuries, by the slave gangs' worksongs and the negro congregations' responses to countless sermons. The sleeve-notes on a number of gospel albums quote from *The Autobiography Of An Ex-Colored Man*, by novelist James Weldon Johnson, in which, referring to the camp-meetings of his youth, he describes 'the solitary and plaintive voice of the leader' being 'answered by a sound like the roll of the sea.'[9] It has been said that because, during the 18th century, blacks were unable to read, each church hired a 'reader' so that the congregation would learn to repeat the words he read out, thereby establishing more deeply the pattern of chant and response which had already been imported from Africa. Today, The Reverend David Robinson's recent recordings for Jewel[10] demonstrate that antiphonal patterns remain solidly rooted in everyday negro church service and are an effective means by which to provoke fervent worship. After delivering the introduction to his sermon with a gentle intonation, the preacher becomes more emphatic and the spoken word gains a rhythmic pulse. The congregation are unable to restrain their desire to shout out in affirmation, and, as the preacher gradually becomes more and more ecstatic, he shifts key and the congregation bursts into song. The use of antiphony is now common throughout the entire field of popular music, notably since Atlantic's promotion men turned Ray Charles's *What I'd Say* (Atlantic 2031) into a million-selling record in 1959.

When discussing the changes that occur in blues styles Keil also observed that 'singers make greater use of melisma (more than one note per syllable), especially in recent years since the gospel influence on blues singing has become more marked'. He thought it 'derived directly from the intensely emotional services of the negro fundamentalist churches' but its foundation lay in the 17th century when slaves learned the hymns, chants and psalms of our colonial forefathers in a slow, drawn-out manner. Notes that were held too long to be sung in one breath were broken and eventually replaced by a quavering line. I can only assume that the effect was immensely attractive, for it remained throughout two hundred years of church singing, and today the black vocalists who use melisma most are also the most popular in the Hit Parade.

Some are able to jump octaves or juggle keys in the space of a syllable. Jackie Wilson, who replaced McPhatter in The Dominoes, is possibly the most accomplished. In *Danny Boy* (Brunswick 55277, a 1958 recording) Wilson compresses over twenty-two notes into the monosyllable 'for'. When Bobby Hendricks toured Britain with the Original Drifters the veins in his neck stood out and visibly quivered at the exertion required to stretch 'only you' over more notes than the two words would seem to accommodate. A close parallel may be drawn with the preacher's stutter, a device employed to convince a congregation that mere words are insufficient to express the speaker's tremendous emotion. McPhatter is equally adept, particularly in those performances which are taken at a slow tempo –

... su-u-um-da-ai-yee you'll wont me-ee-ee
to wo-oh-ont yoo-oo-eh ...

In these days of blue-eyed soul, melisma is a reliable indicator of racial origin. Of all the Caucasians who have tried to imitate the mannerism only Bobby Hatfield of The Righteous Brothers has succeeded – and he only partially. The rest sound gauche and entirely graceless.

Over eight years before *Oh Happy Day*, McPhatter recorded a gospel song for the popular market entitled *I Can't Stand Up Alone* (Atlantic 1199). The lyrics are oblique but the mood of the song clearly refers to a supernatural support without which the singer would lose his sense of balance. A female chorus chants the title and the instrumentation is full. This may have been the first real attempt at 'pop gospel' or it may have been a deliberate dilution of the genuine article, devised to avoid total neglect by pop radio stations. Whatever the motive, *I Can't Stand Up Alone* found its way into over a million homes, coupled with the Brook Benton–Jimmy Williams hit song *A Lover's Question*. Recorded in 1958 after McPhatter had left the Drifters, it was to be the last occasion on which he or they returned to their gospel roots in quite so revealing a fashion.

Bill Pinkney taking a break.

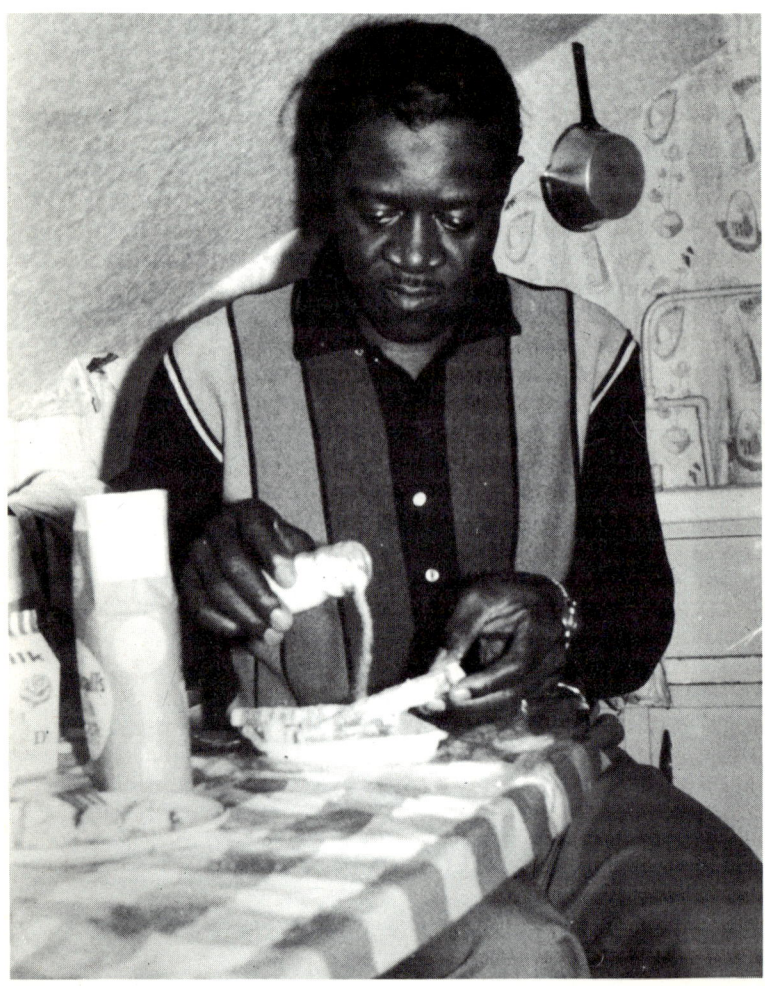

ORNITHOLOGY

> I like coffee, I like tea,
> but I don't like sitting on a black man's knee...

This unfriendly verse, heard throughout English primary schools twenty years ago, may not have been a corruption of *Java Jive* (Decca 3432) as popularised by The Inkspots. I am informed, however, that their recording gave it considerable impetus – which is some indication of their world-wide appeal. They were not the first black vocal group to sing popular music. The Mills Brothers were heard on a national radio network in 1931 and had achieved a million sales with *Tiger Rag* (Decca 1-707) a year before. Others, including The Charioteers, The Delta Rhythm Boys, The Four Knights, The Deep River Boys and The Four Tunes (alias The Sentimentalists) were popular in the United States during the '30s and '40s. But during this period The Inkspots were the most significant group.

Pioneers! From Cashbox, *1947.*

DEEP RIVER BOYS
20-2397 BLOOP BLEEP
I LEFT MYSELF WIDE OPEN

DELTA RHYTHM BOYS WITH FRANK COMSTOCK AND HIS ORCHESTRA
20-2365
EVERY SO OFTEN
COME IN OUT OF THE RAIN

Bill Kenny (lead tenor), Charles Fuqua (second tenor, guitar, ukulele), Deek Watson (baritone, guitar) and Orville 'Hoppy' Jones (bass) first recorded for Victor in New York City during February 1935. For five years they pursued a hot jazz policy, recording titles like *Stompin' At The Savoy* (Decca 1036) and the aforementioned *Java Jive*. In 1939, however, their treatment of *If I Didn't Care* (Decca 23632) virtually divorced them from jazz and began a prolific output of carefully chosen ballads. From the beginning their records for Victor and Decca were issued in Britain, and the 'Family Favourites' appeal of the lyrics of such well-known tunes as *Whispering Grass* (Decca 23632), *I'll Never Smile Again* (Decca 23635) or *We'll Meet Again* (Decca 25237) meant as much to the homesick soldier as did Vera Lynn – who also recorded the last title.

Their greatest strength lay in the nostalgia and melancholy which a war-weary population found comforting; but there was more for the discerning listener. It seemed as though every second recording had an identical introductory guitar cadence, at the end of which Bill Kenny would begin to sing in a tenor-to-falsetto voice as clear as that of a choirboy. He rolled his r's and emphasised other consonants normally lost in popular balladeering. On some of The Inkspots' most memorable successes, Kenny's impeccable diction provided a sharp, novel contrast to the verses spoken by Hoppy Jones. The latter's dark brown voice was superficially lazy, but could be questioning, as in *Do I Worry* (Decca 23633), or, if necessary, emphatic. Kenny's beautiful singing set a pattern for all future tenor leads, while Jones's was the archetypal 'talking bass' much copied in later years. The fact that these two men could, within a single unit, present the gamut of human voices from bass to virtual soprano, in an attractive fashion, enabled them to be more successful than the commonplace white barbershop quartets which were unable to offer such a wide range. In addition, they established, if not introduced, what was to become a standard pattern for the majority of black vocal quartets. The baritone, bass and second tenor would harmonise an accompaniment to the primary vocal line, which relied chiefly upon a tenor lead, or occasionally – usually for novelty – a bass lead. After 1945, groups rarely sang in unison unless they were white. (The Coasters were one of the very few successful exceptions.) The curious, high-pitched but unobtrusive harmony of The Inkspots would not have been anachronistic ten years later; it was but one of the elements in black group singing which became known as rhythm and blues in the '50s, and, more than any other black group of the time, they initiated a stream of development which led in turn to The Ravens, The Orioles, The Dominoes and The Drifters.

The Inkspots appeared at the London Palladium in 1948, but Hoppy Jones had died four years earlier. The nostalgia they had peddled so successfully was no longer necessary. The original group disbanded but

The Inkspots.

gave rise to many other similarly named quartets, some of which still exist today. With the passing of the real Inkspots popular music was sorely deprived of listenable or worthwhile influences until 1953.

The totally independent market for rhythm and blues, however, thrived on the talents of a fresh generation – a generation whose forebears had moved from Mississippi and Carolina to the ghettoes of Oakland, San Francisco, Harlem, New York, and Chicago's South Side. For teenagers like Clyde McPhatter, Sonny Til or Jimmy Ricks life was a struggle they had not invited. When one examines the biographies of these and other black performers it is abundantly clear that, had they not become successful as singers, they would still be engaged in menial employment whatever their ability. There were few careers other than sport and crime. If they did not become boxers (like Roy Hamilton, Jackie Wilson, Jay Hawkins) they bell-hopped (Phil Phillips, Oscar Toney, Eddie Giles) or washed dishes (Lou Rawls, Little Richard Penniman), sold cars (Bill Pinkney) or stole them (James Brown). Deprived of a more meaningful existence, every group of teenagers who sang together on a street corner could attain success of a kind. Success in financial terms was statistically rare, but the gratification achieved by way of self-fulfilment, idle pleasure or fleeting recognition was no less important. Already acquainted with the enjoyment afforded by singing with others in church, countless young blacks formed singing teams at school or in the college 'glee' club. After school or work, they perfected their style and their harmony in the hope of securing a recording contract. Naturally enough, not all those who tried to sing – not even some of the successful ones – could in fact do so. Some sang lead because they were incapable of harmonising; others were simply tone deaf. This is not to say that the results were devoid of charm, feeling or involvement – qualities which similarly inferior white singers found it difficult to provide.

Perhaps because equal rights were not accorded to blacks in general, teenage girls enjoyed even fewer opportunities. While white female singing groups were abundant, of their black counterparts only The Teen Queens, The Chantels, The Bobbettes, The Quintones, The Hearts and an occasional female lead in a largely male group like The Mellows or The Sixteens enjoyed any real success. From the outset the group sound was dominated by male singers.

In 1951 and 1952, black songstress Savannah Churchill and The Mills Brothers scored Top Ten successes in the popular market with *Sin* (Victor 4280) and *Glow-worm* (Decca 28384) respectively. A little later, white singers Johnny Ray and Bill Haley enjoyed popular hits with *Cry* (OKeh 6840) and *Crazy, Man Crazy* (Essex 321), both of which were performed in approximately black styles. Popular music of the time also offered examples of the cover record – a bowdlerisation of R&B performed by whites. (Both Ray and Haley later succumbed to the practice; Ray with The Drifters' *Such A Night* and Haley with Joe Turner's *Shake, Rattle And Roll*.) This phenomenon was later to assume enormous proportions.

During the period under discussion mainstream popular music, whether stolen from blacks or not, was performed by artists of three types. There were jolly female singers, urbane orchestra leaders, and virile balladeers with lungs of leather or shot silk. The Top Twenty was rarely without Kay Starr, Rosemary Clooney or Patti Page; Hugo Winterhalter or Mantovani; Eddie Fisher, Frankie Laine or Tony Bennett. In Britain the story was no different – Norman Wisdom, Dickie Valentine, David Whitfield and Vera Lynn ruled 'showbiz' and the best-selling record charts. British teenagers suffered longer than their American counterparts; when rock 'n' roll began to make an impact in Europe we had heard nothing of its folk model, the R&B vocal group, which in the late '40s and early '50s made what many regard as the only interesting popular music of the period. Followers of Tin Pan Alley or Denmark Street gazed upon a broad spectrum of novelty songs and show tunes, neo-country-and-western ballads and plagiarised, diluted rhythm and blues. It was primarily designed to appeal to everyone from eight to eighty and, while it may have done so, the result was a mish-mash of crass tastelessness, devoid of roots, atmosphere or authenticity. Something had to happen and, fortunately, 'The Sound of the Birds' materialised.

The names of many of the earliest black groups reflected not only the aspirations of their audience but the sweet and refined nature of their material. In many ways it was simply another version of Tin Pan Alley, but, whilst their songs explored the joys or vicissitudes of romance, the lead vocal and harmonic support were appropriately soft, sweet, delicate and, above all, worth listening to. But those who sang in this intimate fashion were still black and, although nothing could be further from the truth, white programme directors called it 'jungle music' – a description they happily applied to all R&B in their initially successful attempts to justify their reasons for ignoring it. Sophistication was occasionally thrown to the wind, but more often the titles which groups gave themselves reflected a preoccupation with romance (The Lovers, The Dreamers, The Moonglows), nobility and royalty (The Coronets, The Barons, The Five Crowns, The Four Kings) or, most effectively, the names of birds.

Many birds sing in a gentle, continuous, trilling manner, and the phrase 'to sing like a bird' has been used to describe all kinds of utterance, from that made by human beings to the inarticulate, if melodious, whistling of a kettle or the wind. By choosing the name of a bird, an enormous number of black vocal groups indicated, by simple connotation, that the listener would find their own singing as attractive as that of the species whose name they adopted. Others were content that their sound should resemble the vocal characteristics of a specific bird, whether it was tuneful or not. The song of the raven, for instance, is no more than a guttural croak, but the group which, in 1946, called itself The Ravens did so appropriately enough, for their lead singer, Jimmy Ricks, had the deepest lead bass in the whole of group R&B. Often groups had the good sense to choose a species which sang sweetly, and if The Larks were already successful, a name which included the vital component was duly invented – thus The Gaylarks, The Lark-Tones and The Meadow-Larks. Other groups were not so pedantic; for them the mere name of a species – any species – was enough. The pleasant lead tenor of The Crows bore no aural resemblance to the coarse cry of that bird. Then, thinking perhaps that they would be worth watching as well as listening to, many groups picked on an exotic species which, though virtually mute, had bright vivid plumage – hence The Flamingos, The Cardinals, The Blue-Jays, The Penguins and The Pelicans. The practice spread to include any creature or thing that buzzed, whined, yelped, howled or rustled; thus there were The Spaniels, The Hornets, The Four Winds, The Bees, The Five Satins and The Crickets. Two more successful groups of the era, The Feathers and The Spiders, simply reinforced identification with the animal kingdom.

The Ravens and The Orioles, formed in 1945 and 1947 respectively, were the first of the 'bird' groups and proved to be the most influential during the next decade. The Ravens, popularly referred to as 'The

Above: *Jimmy Ricks*.
Right: *Sonny Til and the Orioles*.

Grandaddy of R&B groups', grew around Jimmy Ricks and Warren Suttles, who sang along to records, particularly those of The Delta Rhythm Boys, on the jukebox in a tavern where they worked as waiters. Ricks (bass) and Suttles (baritone) recruited a first tenor in Ollie Jones and a second lead vocal in Leonard Puzey. They were signed to Ben Bart's Hub label in 1946 and followed Nat King Cole and Stan Kenton on an Apollo Theater programme during the same year. *Old Man River* (National 9035), their second record for National in 1947, established them in the black market and is reputed to have sold a million copies. It was the first in a series of records on which arrangers Howard Biggs and

Bill Sanford adapted other well-worn standards as showcases for Ricks's unique bass voice.

Whereas, in gospel groups, the family was (and frequently still is) the basic unit, secular groups were prone to constant changes of personnel. The Travelling Echoes, The Porter Family of Los Angeles and The Staples Singers bear witness to the unity which a belief in God encourages. Gertrude Ward continued to sing in the group led with world-wide success by her daughter Clara, and Thomas Johnson and his son Ellis are both in The Harmonizing Four. 'The Sons of the Birds' (the offspring of The Dixie Hummingbirds) have carried this tradition a stage further. Among secular vocal groups, however, instability was at all times a central social factor in their rise to prominence. Thus, in the eleven years of their existence, The Ravens recorded for eight different labels, recruiting at various times as many as nine or more members.[1]

While The Ravens remained moderately successful with black record buyers until the mid-'50s, it was The Orioles who made the significant break into the white record market, with *Crying In The Chapel*. Jesse Walker even attributes the birth of rhythm and blues to them:

> It all started in October 1948 with the arrival in New York from Baltimore of a bright new group known as Sonny Til and The Orioles. These five youngsters arrived at the front door of the Apollo Theater in an old dilapidated 1934 Ford ... Touched by their plight, Mr Schiffman decided to give them a chance and added them to the show which opened at The Apollo that Friday. What had been anticipated as a routine week for The Apollo turned into a rousing success as word of the 'new sound' spread like wildfire. It presented a type of musical expression which had not been heard on The Apollo stage before and signalled the opening of a new era in show business.[2]

Walker has not over-dramatised the situation. Sonny Tilghman, a handsome, debonair young negro, was demobbed in 1946. Returning to Baltimore, he formed The Vibranaires, who made their debut, as Sonny Til and The Orioles, on the Natural label with *It's Too Soon To Know* (Natural 5000). The group – Til (lead), George Nelson (baritone and second lead), Alexander Sharp (tenor), Johnny Reed (bass), and Tommy Gaither (guitar) – was immediately heralded, in Natural Records' advertisements in trade journals, as the nation's greatest singing quartet. In 1949 they were voted 5th in a *Cashbox* Best Vocal Combo poll (The Mills Brothers, The Ravens and The Inkspots were 1st, 4th and 6th respectively) but, although *It's Too Soon To Know* (written by their manager Deborah Chessler) had soared to the top of the R&B chart in November 1948, The Orioles still appealed to a purely negro market. Three and a half years and thirty-one singles after their first recording, Jubilee (the Natural label re-named) released The Orioles' *Crying In The Chapel* (Jubilee 5122). It epitomised the new musical expression referred to by Walker. The Orioles specialised in simple, sentimental ballads whose fragile melodies hung upon the harmony of the group and the lead singer's sweet, soft and unusually relaxed vocal. The label on the British London issue bears the legend 'vocal with instrumental accompaniment' but, apart from introductory chimes, instrumentation is scarcely discernible. To pick out the piano, bass and lightly strummed guitar demands an almost unacceptable degree of concentration.

It's Too Soon To Know had boosted The Orioles to overnight fame within the black sub-culture; *Tell Me So* (Jubilee 5005) was the sixth best-selling R&B record of 1949 and, in 1950 and 1952, *Forgive And Forget* (5016), *What Are You Doing New Year's Eve* (5017) and *Baby Please Don't Go* (5065) made the R&B Top Ten. Many of their other recordings did not sell well,[3] but one could devote a chapter to statistics about the success of *Crying In The Chapel*. It was the first record to 'go pop' – which is to say that it achieved a sale so far in excess of that attained by the average R&B hit that white people must have bought thousands of copies. In the week when it reached number 1 on the R&B charts, *Crying In The Chapel* occupied 20th position in the popular list. The popularity of the record was evenly spread throughout the country; in Philadelphia, Atlanta, New Orleans, Los Angeles and New York the record was amongst the Top Ten best-selling records. With a few exceptions, white disc-jockeys did not play The Orioles' version. It was never among the twenty most frequently broadcast records in the nation – which indicates that white teenagers had been listening, often surreptitiously, to black radio stations.

It was not the first sign of this trend. Leo Mintz, a Cleveland record store owner, had noticed that R&B records were becoming unusually popular at the beginning of the decade, and he encouraged Alan Freed, a disc-jockey at a local radio station, to feature them in his programme. R&B might have gained large-scale national acceptance without Freed, but he was the catalyst. After he played *Crying In The Chapel* the disc is reputed to have sold 30,000 copies in Cleveland alone the very next day. That so many copies were even available suggests evidence of 'payola' – the officially iniquitous practice whereby disc-jockeys are bribed to play certain songs. In June 1951, after numerous jobs as a sportscaster or programme director on stations in Philadelphia and Ohio, Freed appeared on WJW Cleveland introducing 'Moondog's Rock 'n' Roll Party'. This unlikely looking thirty-year-old white man of Welsh-Lithuanian descent rechristened R&B in order to avoid the racial stigma which he thought was inherent in such a classification. In the lyrics of rhythm and blues material the word 'roll' was synonymous with sexual intercourse whilst 'rock', like 'bop' or 'shake', simply reinforced the rhythm of those records which were designed to be danced to as well as listened to. Freed combined two words which he had heard commonly expressed on the records he played. In doing so he may well have received inspiration from a black group, Billy Mathews and The Balladeers, who had made the title *Rock And Roll* in 1949 (Arlington 201), or even jazz orchestra leader, Joe Haymes, who recorded *Rock And Roll* in 1935 (Conqueror 8447). Morris Levy, head of Roulette records, later recalled:

The way I look at it, all R&B is more popular today because of one guy – Alan Freed. He was actually the first dee-jay to play R&B and Blues on a pop music radio station . . . Freed came up with the term rock 'n' roll for the name of those shows. We copyrighted the term. And we actually collected royalties from record companies for its use. But then we couldn't protect it after a while, about two weeks, because it would have meant filing a thousand lawsuits.[4]

Before the success of *Crying In The Chapel* Freed, prompted by his abnormally large listening figures, had staged a Moondog Rock 'n' Roll

Ball in the 10,000-capacity Cleveland Arena in March 1952. Thirty-thousand showed up and riots caused the event to be cancelled. Freed was surprised to find that a substantial minority of the disappointed audience was white. In 1955 he staged two more shows: one at St Nicholas Arena in January and a second, featuring The Penguins and The Moonglows, at The Brooklyn Paramount during Easter. At the first, Freed himself observed the audience to be 70% white and 30% black.

Despite a serious car-crash in April 1953, in which he nearly lost his life, Freed revolutionised the entire record industry within the space of three years. His affection for black music had long been apparent; as a youth in Salem, Ohio, he had organised a Dixieland jazz group and called them The Sultans of Swing after a black Harlem band. Later, he had no truck with disc-jockeys who preferred the pale imitation cover records. He likened them to racialists – 'If it isn't that, what is it? Oh, they can always excuse it on the ground that the covers are better quality recordings, but I defy anyone to show me that the quality of the original *Tweedlee Dee* or *Seven Days*[5] or any of those others is poor.'[6] Freed did not have to play The Orioles' recording of *Crying In The Chapel*. It was not even the original recording; when they entered the charts two country and western singers, including the composer, Artie Glenn, and a girl vocalist, June Valli, already had hits with the same tune. Considerations of bribery aside, Freed played The Orioles' version because he thought black music was honest.[7]

As far as black vocal groups were concerned the hitherto unprecedented success of *Crying In The Chapel* opened Pandora's box. Within the next few months, another five records made the cross-over from R&B to national success in the best-selling Top Twenty. Significantly, all were by groups and, since they were not necessarily enormous hits in the R&B market, it is logical to assume that whites were initially more impressed by those R&B records which were less obviously of black origin. *Gee* (Rama 5) by The Crows reached the Top Twenty in April 1954 but was never higher than 6th in the black market, whilst *I Understand* by The Four Tunes (Manor 1093), a top-twenty hit in May, was only a minor R&B success. Indeed, The Crows and The Four Tunes may have been amongst the first black groups whose records are likely to have been produced with the white audience in mind. Even *Crying In The Chapel*, although on the popular charts for ten weeks, was not in the top three best-selling R&B records of 1953. Those that were – by Ruth Brown, Faye Adams and Willie Mae Thornton – were not hits in the popular market. Much of The Orioles' material had already been successful with whites and Til's voice betrayed little, if any, indication of his social status. He did not possess a readily identifiable negro accent, and whilst white adolescents were aware of buying a black group record it was not accidental that they picked, from amongst the myriads of black groups, those whose voices could almost pass for white.

The success of The Orioles, The Crows, The Four Tunes, The Penguins, The Chords and The Charms in the white market is ample confirmation that the first groups to enjoy bi-racial appeal were those who, by and large, eliminated 'black' vocal mannerisms from their performances. White adolescents may have been ready to accept the less melodic, often risqué, gospel-cum-blues styles of The Clovers, The Five Royales, The Dominoes and The Drifters, but white radio stations were still unwilling, and, without exposure, the groups were not accorded national acclaim unless (or until) they radically altered their performances to suit the tastes of white programme directors.

Accordingly, although *Sh-boom* by The Chords (Cat 104), *Hearts Of Stone* by The Charms (Deluxe 6062) and *Gee* by The Crows were popular hits, they only rated as 12th, 25th and 28th best-selling records in the R&B market during 1954. In comparison, *Honey Love*, *Money Honey* and *Such A Night*, intense gospel-style records by Clyde McPhatter and The Drifters, were 2nd, 11th and 18th best-selling R&B records but were not national hits.

McPhatter was just seventeen years of age when, in 1950, he joined Billy Ward's Dominoes. Ward, pianist, organist, arranger, composer and singing coach recruited a vocal group from amongst his best students in New York City. In addition to James Van Loan (tenor), Joe

The Chords, who changed their name for later releases, were one of the first groups to go 'pop'. From Cashbox, *1954.*

SLEEPER OF THE WEEK

"HOLD ME BABY" (2:20)
[Progressive BMI—Feaster, McRae, Edwards, Keyes]

"A GIRL TO LOVE" (2:57)
[Progressive BMI—Feaster]

THE CHORDCATS
(Cat 112)

THE CHORDCATS

● The Chordcats have a pair of potent decks on this latest release. A jump, "Hold Me Baby", and a pretty blues ballad, "A Girl To Love". The first is an energetic effort in which the lads maintain a strong beat that gets under your skin. Both items are good pop possibilities. The arrangements on both sides are not the least of the appeal. Either or both could make their marks.

Lamount (baritone) and Bill Brown (bass) he lured McPhatter away from a full-time clerical job with the promise of a position as lead tenor. The group are chiefly remembered for their succession of talented bass singers, particularly Brown, who sang lead on their first Federal recording *Chicken Blues* (Federal 12001) and the best-selling R&B record of 1951 – *60 Minute Man* (Federal 12022). The second tenor was the brother of Joe and Paul Van Loan of The Ravens, and the reliance upon a bass as lead vocal indicated the debt owed to Jimmy Ricks. (Others included David McNeil on *Pedal Pushing Papa* (Federal 12114) and Cliff Givens on *Can't Do Sixty No More* (Federal 12209).) Despite their stylistic and familial relationship with The Ravens, The Dominoes' producer Ralph Bass was reluctant to allow McPhatter's gospel training to go unnoticed. Besides *The Bells*, McPhatter sang lead on many of the twenty-two Federal singles including *Have Mercy Baby* (Federal 12068) which was Number One on the R&B chart in June 1952 and the second largest R&B record of that year. Over a decade later, Bass produced the pop gospel of The Violinaires and The Harold Smith Majestic Choir to whom passing reference was made in the previous chapter.

Jackie Wilson, who replaced McPhatter in The Dominoes, recently talked of his two-year apprenticeship prior to McPhatter's departure: 'I fell in love with the man's voice. I toured with the group and watched Clyde and listened; finally I got a chance to join the group'.[8] Wilson's opportunity arose in 1953, when McPhatter left The Dominoes[9] and, with encouragement from Lou Krefetz who had discovered and managed The Clovers, formed a group of his own: The Drifters.

Dependence upon a manager, producer or agent (inevitably a man older than the group and its audience) was a natural development throughout the decade. Buck Ram, who managed The Platters, also wrote many of their best-selling records, and Esther Navarro performed a similar dual function for The Cadillacs. The arrangement enabled each group to maintain an easily identifiable style. McPhatter and his fellow Dominoes had previously turned to Billy Ward and producer Ralph Bass for the expertise which they lacked. Now, on Atlantic, McPhatter asked Sarah Vaughan's husband and manager, George Treadwell, to manage his new group. In addition, the other members gave up their jobs to place themselves wholeheartedly at the record company's disposal. They relied upon Atlantic's producers for the choice, arrangement and authorship of their material. Half of the titles made by McPhatter and The Drifters were written and arranged by Jerry Wexler, Tom Dowd and Ahmet Ertegun. Dowd, a pioneer in recording techniques, had already engineered recordings by The Ravens, who were the first of the 'bird' groups.

The circumstances surrounding The Drifters' formation have recently been contradicted by Jerry Wexler who assured readers[10] that McPhatter had been signed to Atlantic by his partner, Ahmet Ertegun, in

Jackie Wilson replaced Clyde McPhatter in The Dominoes and ultimately became a big solo attraction.

the same week that McPhatter left The Dominoes. Although the first Drifters' recordings had been made two months earlier, *Billboard* did not report McPhatter's split with The Dominoes until their late-September issue. Johnny Parker, who wrote the reverse of The Drifters' first release and took notes at the Atlantic recording dates he attended, gave the personnel as McPhatter, Gerhart Thrasher (tenor), Charlie Hughes (baritone) and Bill Pinkney (bass). On numerous later occasions, McPhatter both corroborated and refuted Parker's statements, but others, including Thrasher, believed his brother, Andrew, to be present in place of Hughes. Another version offered the possibility that Willie Ferbee initially sang bass and was replaced by Bill Pinkney on The Drifters' second session. Wexler has also referred to an occasion, before July 1953, when different group members were used for a mediocre session which had to be discarded. I mention such contradictions as an illustration of the frenzied activity when the acceleration to form groups was equalled only by the haste of record companies to sign them.

At the suspicion of a record contract, many a young hopeful would assemble his buddies and return down-town to audition for 'Big Max' who operated the local label. If his friends were not available, he spread the word around his block, the streets or the pool-hall, in his anxiety to recruit anyone rather than lose the opportunity to make a record. This partly explains how it is possible to question ex-members of innumerable vocal groups at length, only to be faced with several identical claims, counter-claims and fabrication. Many groups who gathered in a studio did not even know each other's names.

The Drifters' association with Atlantic continues today, yet the label also had other black groups – The Regals, The Diamonds, The Rockets and The Crescendoes – all of whom are now totally unknown. Whilst a contract with The Apollo Theater, which will be discussed later, made an immeasurable contribution to The Drifters' endurance, talent was another important factor. They were more versatile than their contemporaries, and the first records they made were particularly good. Officially, only six singles of Clyde McPhatter and The Drifters were released: all were Top Ten rhythm and blues hits between September 1953 and June 1955. Appendix 2 illustrates the success of each Drifters recording in both popular and R&B markets. Within this period, only two groups, The Clovers and The Midnighters, rivalled The Drifters' popularity with black listeners. During 1953, each had three records in the R&B Top Ten simultaneously, but this phenomenal success was not sustained. The Drifters' *Money Honey* began a remarkable string of hit records which, for consistency over a period of thirteen years, has yet to be surpassed by any group in recording history.

Unsophisticated recording techniques will forever link the first six records to the period in which they were made, but no selection of six

★ AWARD O' THE WEEK ★

"YOUR CASH AIN'T NOTHIN' BUT TRASH" (2:51)
[Progressive BMI—Calhoun]

"I'VE GOT MY EYES ON YOU" (2:28)
[Progressive BMI—Winley]

THE CLOVERS
(Atlantic 1035)

THE CLOVERS

● The Clovers, who make a habit of coming up with two hit releases, look like they may do it again with their latest, "Your Cash Ain't Nothin' But Trash" and "I've Got My Eyes On You". The "Cash" side is a middle tempo bounce novelty with a humorous set of lyrics that is bound to appeal. The group is getting smoother with each release but retains that infectious appeal that marks all of their decks. The flip, "Eyes", is a quick tempo, Calypso beat, jump item that the boys knock out with a zestful performance. It's heads or tails on this platter. It could be either or both for the charts.

★ AWARD O' THE WEEK ★

"STINGY LITTLE THING" (2:47)
[Armo BMI—Henry Ballard]

"TELL THEM" (2:02)
[Armo BMI—Sonny Woods]

THE MIDNIGHTERS
(Federal 12202)

THE MIDNIGHTERS

● The Midnighters have dropped "Annie" for this release. The lads, however, seem to do well enough without their patron saint. They have an infectious bouncer titled "Stingy Little Thing". Ditty is a story of the gal who is so stingy with her loving. The Midnighters have developed into a fine singing group and the results are apparent on this wax. The flip, "Tell Them", is a slow sad romantic blues beautifully performed. The wailing lead tells his tale with feeling and the others back him effectively. Two good sides.

The Clovers and The Midnighters were the only groups to rival The Drifters in popularity with black listeners. From Cashbox, *1954.*

later recordings achieves such a wide variety of sounds and styles. In less than a year, The Drifters shouted defiance in mock gospel, swung Latin-American rhythms in *Honey Love*, and expressed their innermost thoughts of romance in the gentle but intricate harmony typical of the ornithologically inspired groups. Three years before the mass promotion of rock 'n' roll by whites, The Drifters also made *Money Honey* – now an accepted rock 'n' roll classic.

To infuse each diverse musical tradition with the same brilliant quality says much for McPhatter's intuitive vocal gifts. 'He was and is,' said Wexler, 'one of the great and unique soul singers of all time.' There are differences between the 'new' soul and the 'old' R&B that Wexler ignored. When McPhatter sighs in *Honey Love* or screams in *Whatcha*

Bill Pinkney in action.

Gonna Do the effect is one of spontaneity. There are none of the boring formulas and carefully calculated clichés from which the 'new' soul so very often suffers. Apart from *Honey Love*, McPhatter rarely wrote songs; it was not necessary. It is difficult to believe that some of the standards The Drifters recorded had an existence independent of him, for his interpretation gave each song an entirely new slant. The heavily corrugated nature of his opening phrase and the unexpected emphasis on certain syllables creates a new melody out of *White Christmas*. His high, naturally exuberant voice adds an exciting quality quite alien to the sober Tin Pan Alley renditions of the same tune. McPhatter had discovered his powers of improvisation some years before: 'We were very frightened in the studio when we were recording ... Billy Ward was teaching us the song and he said "sing it up" and I said, "well, I don't feel it that way" and he said "try it your way". I felt more relaxed if I wasn't confined to the melody. I would take liberties with it and he'd say, "that's great, do it that way".'[11]

Although The Drifters featured an amalgam of styles over a wide period of time, the influence of the 'bird' groups was never apparent after 1958 and can only be satisfactorily explained by reference to certain of the titles made during McPhatter's residence as lead singer. The physically exhausting evening suggested in his lascivious vocal on *Such A Night* would have been casually understated by the gentle voice of Sonny Til; while the full instrumentation of many of The Drifters' early recordings was not a marked feature of The Orioles, The Ravens or other 'bird' groups. But the appeal of *Someday* and *White Christmas* did rely, in part, on the bass taking a verse from the tenor lead, just as Bill Kenny and Hoppy Jones swopped verses in The Inkspots, or George Nelson of The Orioles took a verse from Sonny Til in *It's Too Soon To Know*.

Gone and *The Way I Feel* (originally a hit for The Four Knights) were respectively the first and third songs The Drifters recorded. (*Lucille*, made in between, is very slow and beautifully sung, but the group, who chant rather than harmonise, create a pronounced and deliberate beat.) These two records were made in July and August 1953, just as The Orioles' recording of *Crying In The Chapel* was making a national impact. As a result, both performances displayed the mood, mannerisms and content matter which separated the 'bird' groups from all other forms of R&B.

Instrumentation exists, but purely in a subordinate role. Ben Webster's soft saxophone breathes gently behind the lead singer on *The Way I Feel*, and there is a one-note piano introduction from Van Walls. There is no break for any kind of instrumental passage and McPhatter is occasionally unaccompanied by instrument or human voice. Nothing diverts the listener's attention from the vocalist who, although he has some of the mannerisms of Sonny Til, is more emotional, and quietly chokes when approaching the end of a sentence. When The Drifters continued without McPhatter, the quiet, intense harmonic exercises of the 'bird' group were replaced by different, if equally enjoyable, vocal techniques. The unobtrusive musical accompaniment to their first sessions together enables the harmony of The Drifters to be heard to an advantage which was seldom repeated in later years. One can find that listening to their combination of gently wavering falsetto cries, assorted 'doo wahs' and a curious burping effect from the bass singer is a delicious experience – or no more than comical. Whatever one's response, it is difficult not to marvel at the rapport achieved when the singers were likely to have been thrust together only hours before they entered the recording studio. Critics persistently and correctly refer to the 'polished' harmony of black vocal groups without realising that many were formed overnight, which bears testimony to the rhythmic sense of those who complemented the lead singer.

The Way I Feel and *Gone* were written by Johnny Parker and Eloise Hinds respectively. Parker had been a successful crooner for a number of years and consequently *The Way I Feel* is a trite, self-conscious ballad typical of Tin Pan Alley. The singer feels bad because his lover is not returning; he is able to savour only the remembrance of a sweet thrill or tender embrace. *Gone* has identical sentiments and both are slow laments whose primary purpose was to serve a youthful audience who held lights-out parties, clutched their girl friends close and danced cheek to cheek in a fashion in keeping with the funereal tempo of the record.

The Atlantic label had no wish to lose its new and exciting acquisition amongst the numerous and often almost indistinguishable groups who specialised in the extremely competitive harmony style. Accordingly, apart from *White Christmas*, the songs in which The Drifters displayed a penchant for close harmony and spiritually captured 'The Sound of the Birds' were not promoted as hit material. *Gone*, the result of their first session in July 1953, was not released until 1955 and then only as a flip-side. *The Way I Feel*, made a month after *Gone*, was tucked away on the reverse of *Money Honey*, which topped the R&B chart for ten weeks towards the end of 1953.

Everyone's Laughing, the first recording to be promoted as a solo by Clyde McPhatter, had 'vocal quartet' printed on the label. These anonymous gentlemen were, in fact, The Drifters, but they were not permitted to shine vocally. The singer sounds more self-conscious than ever; what hurts him most is not the fact that his girl has left him or even that everyone knows about it. What destroys him is that they should find his situation humorous. The full accompaniment, including a rasping tenor saxophone solo, entirely fails to complement the mood. The record gave some indication of the way in which group R&B was moving. It was made in 1955, three years after *Gone* and *The Way I Feel*.

ROCKIN' 'N' DRIFTIN'

The Drifters made nineteen songs between 1955 and 1958. As a result of Atlantic's entry into the white popular music market, ten of these were up-tempo; mostly torrid twelve-bar blues with a piano or 'booting' tenor solo. Fast or slow, they were songs composed by the household names of rock 'n' roll: Leiber and Stoller (who wrote The Coasters' biggest hits); Buck Ram (who did the same for The Platters); Otis Blackwell (song-writer-in-chief for Elvis Presley) and Norman Petty (who collaborated on Buddy Holly compositions). There were others not quite so well known: multi-instrumentalist Buddy Lucas, rock 'n' roller Chuck Willis, and Jesse Stone, who is rumoured to have composed, under the pseudonym of Charles Calhoun, many rock 'n' roll hits, including *Shake, Rattle And Roll*.

The impact of the arrival of rock 'n' roll and, in particular, its effect upon the black vocal group was enormous. It destroyed some and brought momentary fame to others. Apart from The Drifters, very few outlived it. By 1955, although a number of small independents continued to refer to their output as R&B, the rest of the world called it rock 'n' roll. Alan Freed's popularity had reached New York, where he had needed little persuasion to join WINS for $25,000 a year. 'Moondog' was dropped and his show simply became 'Rock 'n' Roll Party'. Established black performers including Fats Domino and Joe Turner were happy to find that they were rock 'n' rollers. The music played by these – and similarly pleased but bewildered veterans of R&B – did not radically change as a result of Freed's new nomenclature. The lyrics, however, had now to be addressed to a young generation and not a particular race.

Some black solo performers proved to be versatile, but most established groups were unable to adapt their presentation in order to survive.

They had invented and popularised a form of R&B unlike any other. In one respect it was far too gentle and sophisticated to pass for rock 'n' roll and its practitioners were no longer accepted by the young and now predominantly white audience for whom the fresh classification existed. After *Crying In The Chapel*, The Orioles did attempt a number of modifications. Their staunchest admirers noted the change which habitually follows commercial success. There was less of a bluesy quality and a greater concentration upon popular songs and quasi-religious offerings like *In The Mission Of St Augustine* (Jubilee 5127). Til sang more emphatically and indulged in tricky changes of tempo. The musical accompaniment increased from the occasional violin in 1950 through the saxophone of Buddy Lucas in 1952 to the full orchestras of Lee Lovett and Sid Bass in 1955. But the success of *Crying In The Chapel* was not repeated. Throughout the last decade, Til has hopped from label to label on his own or with a new group of Orioles, but always without success. It is sad to relate that he was later asked, by the more selfish among record collectors, to refrain from re-recording his old songs for fear of devaluing the inflated prices accorded to his original versions.[1]

The Ravens marginally outlasted The Orioles but also fell by the wayside. Warren Suttles left to form The Dreamers with the specific intention of obtaining the sound of a white pop group from a black quartet and Maithe Marshall and Leonard Puzey returned to obscurity later to re-emerge in one of the numerous groups who called themselves The Inkspots. Ricks made a long list of fine but unsuccessful records for various little companies. The 'birds' had flown.

New groups took their place. Other singers, less heavily influenced by the church, the blues or Tin Pan Alley, formed a new breed with an entirely different sound. The music was boisterous and gimmick-ridden and the new stylists were younger – in many cases, very young indeed. The lyrics were invariably aimed at the adolescent section of society from which the individual group members came. Material for them was provided by the life-situations of the average lower-class American teenager. Romance was now set in a high-school context. 'The most popular subject', said Delehant, 'was undoubtedly girl-friends; the songs eulogised kissing them, breaking up, going back, holding them, dancing with them. Romance was "from the corner candy store to the chapel on the hill" and true love was found in "the way you hold my hand and the way you comb your hair." Better yet, true love was the wonder of "making love by juke-box light".'[2] Other characteristics of the juvenile world were common. The Coasters sold millions with a series of records that described a variety of teenage activities and pleasures in a dead-pan, humorous fashion. They got hot and bothered over watching girls in *Young Blood* (Atco 6087); featured low-key anti-parental protest in *Yakety Yak* (Atco 6116); satirised the Western

TV hero in *Along Came Jones* (Atco 6141); fell about and grew hilarious explaining the mildly delinquent adventures of *Charlie Brown* (Atco 6132). Carrying books to school, flash cars, being sent to bed early and high-school rings were inextricably mixed into the new lyric formulae. The Monotones pointed to the generation gap in a single couplet:

> Just because they do not understand,
> Be-bop-shi-bi-di-lee-bop bip-bam!

And, in the same song – *Tom Foolery* (Argo 5301) – adult pleasures were neatly ridiculed:

> Who wants to waltz and minuet,
> Two hundred years ago, you bet!

Concentration upon lyrics which communicated solely with an adolescent audience and, in many instances, rejected parental values now had a doubly important function. Besides the commercial appeal to a teenaged group which had never had so much money before and had never had a musical genre it could truly call its own, the songs could no longer be copied by older, white artists.

By the mid-'50s, the practice of covering the record of a black group by stealing the arrangement and placing it in the hands of various established homely-looking white performers was yielding fabulous rewards. Study of the Top Ten nation-wide best-selling records on 12 March 1955 shows no less than six eviscerated R&B tunes performed by white artists. The original black recording is shown in parentheses:[3]

(1)	*Sincerely*	McGuire Sisters	(Moonglows – Chess 1581)
(3)	*Tweedlee Dee*	Georgia Gibbs	(Lavern Baker – Atlantic 1047)
(5)	*Kokomo*	Perry Como	(Gene and Eunice – Combo 64, Aladdin 3276)
(7)	*Hearts of Stone*	Fontaine Sisters	(Jewels – R&B 1301)
(8)	*Earth Angel*	Crewcuts	(Penguins – Dootone 348)
(10)	*Kokomo*	Crewcuts	(See no. 5)

Unlike the hegemony of white groups of Italian extraction during the early '60s or the later blue-eyed soul shouters, this first generation of counterfeiters had no respect for the essentials of R&B. Georgia Gibbs, who built her career by recording and subsequently diluting R&B originals, readily changed the lyrics of the songs she copied in order to avoid sexual references. *Roll With Me Henry*, a hit in the negro market for Etta James, under the title of *Wallflower* (Modern 947), became *Dance With Me Henry* when performed by a white woman for a white audience: Etta James' version sold 400,000, Georgia Gibbs sold one million. Situations expressed in songs by The Moonglows or The Spaniels lost their complexity when covered by The McGuire Sisters or The Crewcuts. The latter group, white Canadians, who, apart from their haircuts, had little going for them, sang badly with none of the subtlety that made The Penguins' *Earth Angel* or Gene and Eunice's *Kokomo* more interesting. Bing Crosby, who had covered black hits by Louis Jordan, had the impudence to tell the world that Pat Boone was ruining his voice by attempting to sing R&B. The integrity of black music which had so appealed to Alan Freed was all but destroyed by a handful of ersatz R&B plagiarists. With the advent of teenaged groups who wrote and sang songs which entirely related to their own readily identifiable culture, the impact of the cover record was temporarily weakened. *Earth Angel* was particularly important, for although it did not surpass sales of The Crewcut's version, the original recording brought admirable sales for The Penguins alongside the copyists. Dootsie Williams, President of Dootone records, recalled:

Of course, *Earth Angel* was pop and rhythm and blues; it sold in both fields ... The Crewcuts covered *Earth Angel* too ... They may have sold more than we did because of the advantage the white artists and outlets have over the rhythm and blues outlets. There were about twenty different recordings of it by different artists.[4]

As groups proliferated, the age at which they turned professional became lower than at any previous period. They began to call themselves The Collegians, The Sixteens or The Teen-chords to establish a bond between the group and an audience of the same age. For the first time, black groups made records with little fear of competition from whites. Just how casually an adolescent group could wind up with a million-seller was illustrated by The Monotones first recording:

Book of Love (Argo 5290), we kind of wrote as we were getting out of high school and it came about from a commercial for Pepsodent – 'you'll wonder where the yellow went when you brush your teeth with Pepsodent'. And the drum part that goes 'boom' we got that while we were practising. The kids outside had threw a ball against the window and the ball hit the window the same time as we said 'I wonder who oh who'. And that ball hit the window 'boom' and we played back the tape and we heard this here sound so we kept it in as the drum part. That's what sold the record.[5]

Imitating the sound of an engine in a lyric about a new automobile of which the singer was proud was considered infantile and artists like Perry Como had no wish to proclaim 'I'm not a Juvenile Delinquent'

The Monotones.

even if the tune was an inviting commercial proposition. The solidarity of age and interest between groups and their audience ousted older white performers from the market. Some, including Frank Sinatra and the Bing Crosby already mentioned, attacked rock 'n' roll viciously and in doing so made it more difficult for performers of a similar age and background to continue their habit of covering the music their contemporaries openly denigrated. Perry Como and Georgia Gibbs were set aside as square.

Even if the Tin Pan Alley establishment no longer plagiarised negro tunes, a number of white rock 'n' roll singers became popular and remained popular on the strength of revivals of songs which had been successful in the black market several years before. Presley's *Hound Dog* (Victor 6604) and *Lawdy Miss Clawdy* (Victor 6642) had been R&B hits for Willie Mae Thornton and Lloyd Price, and his phrasing on *White Christmas* was a facsimile of the treatment given to the same tune by Clyde McPhatter and The Drifters. The humour of the situation, brought out by the latter in *Money Honey* was less noticeable in Presley's version (Victor 6641) but, apart from this minor point, Presley was different from older popular singers of the same colour. Unlike the phonies described towards the beginning of this chapter, Presley, who came from Tupelo, Mississippi, had imbibed black musical influences from birth. Like the many exciting white Southerners whose styles, repertoire or both owed varying debts to rhythm and blues, the influence was natural, rather than acquired. No other white artist so consistently dominated the R&B best-sellers and although no black rock 'n' roll idol has achieved similar status, blacks have never begrudged his success. Some, like Little Richard and Jimmy Witherspoon have generously given him credit for his contribution towards de-segregating the national Hit Parade.

However, the economic survival of black groups was not guaranteed by the absence of less worthy cover versions. Black children continued to sing for enjoyment on street corners throughout ghettoes in each of the big cities. Late into the night they harmonised together, sublimating a frustration which, day by day, exploded in gang warfare or less violent activities. The sleeve-note to a Dells album (Buddah 5053) reproduces an article from *Hit Parader* in which their bass singer, Chuck Barksdale, recalled: 'Man, we were stone hooligans. We broke out car windows and threw pumpkins at buses. We were bad, man, but we were always singing.' With his zip-guns and switch-blades safely stored in the cistern of an apartment shared with three other families, a Harlem ten-year-old could leave his decaying tenement and join others similarly unfortunate for an *a capella* session on a deserted subway platform. Street corner talent-spotting became the normal chance for a group to obtain a record contract. An audition from the guy who had crossed the road to listen to them might mean $5000 a week; gifts for the folks back home and a custom-built Cadillac. But many groups were too young to drive or to sign record contracts. Their parents, scarcely knowing what it was all about, signed on junior's behalf. A million seller or a string of dismal failures could follow. It did not matter which, for the group was soon back in the ghetto, tossed aside like an empty cigarette packet. In his article in 'Crawdaddy', Delehant summed up the situation beautifully:

Greasy Joe got his buddies together and they practised a song he wrote about his girl. They practised after school, every night and even in school, perfecting their close harmonies in the high-school men's room. Maybe they got 20 bucks apiece from a record company with a name like Crustation and the next day their song *Emaretta* was on the local charts. Greasy Joe and the Roll Collars were hanging around the corner again one month later, discussing whether or not James Dean busted his fist in *Rebel Without A Cause*.

Greed and exploitation by an inconsiderate management destroyed almost every group which enjoyed a brief taste of fame between 1955 and 1957. The Eldorados, according to the sleeve-note to their album, came into being – like the majority of groups in the mid-'50s – 'on big city street corners and in a dingy pool-room where five or six youngsters with nothing to do harmonised just for kicks.' They had one big hit, *At My Front Door* (VeeJay 147), and five more singles in a similar mould – then nothing. Where are Louis Bradley, James Maddox, Jewel Jones, Richard Nickens and Porkle Lee Moses today?

Tommy White of Lee Andrews and The Hearts now serves other people's hit records to customers at one of New York's biggest record stores, whilst Leroy Griffin, lead vocalist with The Nutmegs, was recently rumoured to have been burned alive in the steel furnace where he worked for the last years of his life. These and many, many more were consigned to obscurity. It is difficult to find a black group member who, having risen to fame in 1955, 1956 or 1957, remains active today. It is almost impossible to find one who is still successful. Frankie Lymon explained why:

All my business transactions were handled by someone else, who hired someone else, who hired someone else . . . They were always careful to keep the kid happy of course. They bought him what he wanted. What did I want? What would any kid of thirteen want? Certainly I didn't want to think about bank accounts and taxes and getting the proper receipts and that sort of thing. They would pat me on the head and tell me how great I was. I was merely a pawn in a big chess game.[6]

Lymon, and his group, The Teenagers, made a greater impact than others during 1956, but their case history and fortunes were typical of the period. His obituary is also familiar. He was born in the tenements of Washington Heights in September 1942 and spent his formative years in a ramshackle apartment with half a dozen relatives. When Quintano's Professional School closed at 4 pm he and a few class-mates sang gospel and tunes they had written themselves in the street. Richard Barrett, lead with the already popular Valentines, heard them and took them along to George Goldner who ran Gee, a subsidiary of Roulette. Their first release, *Why Do Fools Fall In Love* (Gee 1002), propelled The Teenagers from the poverty of a cracked and peeling tenement to $8000 a week. It coincided with the initial mass promotion of rock 'n' roll (Elvis Presley, Little Richard and Carl Perkins had their first Top Ten national best-selling records simultaneously); remained on the chart for four months; topped the British Hit Parade; and sold two million copies throughout the world. Sherman Garnes (bass) aged 15, Joe Negroni (baritone) aged 16, Herman Santiago (first tenor) aged 16, and Jimmy Merchant (second tenor) aged 15, had helped Lymon to embellish the tune which he had written as a poem whilst in the fifth grade. At thirteen, he had bigger problems than his royalties and none of the group had any idea where their money went. They embarked on a continual whirlwind of TV dates, record hops and package tours. Lymon later bemoaned his lack of education:

Kids who sang rock 'n' roll were snatched out of High School because of a hit record. When the success blew over they didn't even have a high school diploma.

For eighteen months it was impossible to live in the USA without hearing The Teenagers. They had other hits including *I'm Not A Juvenile Delinquent* (Gee 1026) but the plea was less convincing when, in the spring of 1957, they appeared at the London Palladium. Lymon swaggered everywhere with a six-inch cigar in his mouth and the group were banished from hotels in London and Manchester for riotous

The Teenagers played to packed houses on their tour of Great Britain in 1957.

behaviour. They split up on return to the USA. Lymon learnt to sing in six languages, took dancing lessons and drummed in a jazz group. His efforts went unnoticed. The rest of the world did not hear of Lymon again until 1964 when it was reported that he had been given bail pending trial on a narcotics charge. On 28 February 1968 he was in the news again. His body had been discovered on the bathroom floor of his grandmother's apartment. A syringe lay beside him. The police at West 153rd Street confirmed that heroin had claimed another life. An international celebrity at thirteen, Frankie Lymon was dead at 26. He was penniless for the last years of his life and the rock 'n' roll era had left him no better off than many contemporaries who had no hit records at all.

As it became harder for whites to imitate black group styles – and hence their records – the major companies ceased to produce cover versions and began to sign the genuine article. The Ravens, Sugar and Spice and The Penguins were snapped up by Mercury – the very same company which prevented The Penguins from securing a monopoly of sales on their original recording of *Earth Angel*. The Penguins' manager, Buck Ram, brought another of his groups – The Platters – to the same company's attention. Mercury's access to white-owned sales outlets and distributors enabled The Platters to escape cover versions almost entirely, even though they had switched from an earthy, unsophisticated form of R&B to a widely acceptable pop ballad sound which white artists could have easily reproduced.[7] In order to compete with the influx of fast novelty recordings by adolescent quartets, other black groups were more often forced to change their style in the opposite direction. Hank Ballard and The Midnighters pointed out the way. In 1952, The Royals made soft sentimental ballads like *Everybeat Of My Heart* (Federal 12064), *Moonrise* (Federal 12088) and *In The Shrine Of St Cecilia* (Federal 12121). In 1954, renamed The Midnighters, the same group made *Work With Me Annie* (Federal 12169) and a string of successful novelty recordings re-working the same theme and featuring repetitious lyrics, solid booting accompaniment and very little melody. Sonny Woods, bass with the group, admitted: 'We didn't practice any of these. If you'll notice they were all done in the same key. About all we did was change the lyrics around.'[8] The Drifters – never without a sense of direction – were soon to follow suit. Weeks before their repertoire had been decisively sweet 'n' greasy; fairly evenly divided between revitalised Tin Pan Alley standards and frantic gospel-cum-blues, both of which found favour with blacks of all ages. From 1955 to the end of the decade, they sang instead about the 'red hot rock 'n' roll beat' and young people, primarily white adolescents, went wild with identification.

Clyde McPhatter's departure had coincided with the decline of the 'bird' groups. Early in 1954, he joined a much larger group – the

United States armed forces – where, like Sonny Til, Lloyd Price and later Elvis Presley, he entertained his fellow soldiers in a division of Special Services. During leave, McPhatter recorded sessions with The Drifters, a duet with Ruth Brown and two solo sessions. The solo recordings, *Seven Days* (Atlantic 1981) and *The Treasure Of Love* (Atlantic 1092), established him as a national favourite prior to his discharge on 19 April 1956. The split with The Drifters was final and here we should leave McPhatter but for one strange anomaly. Record companies do not exist to aid discographers and Atlantic's attitude to releasing the music they have recorded has not helped towards a clear understanding of The Drifters' history. During the late '50s and early '60s, the 'A' or plug side of a new Drifters' record was frequently coupled with a flip or 'B' side which featured previously unissued material recorded several years before. In consequence of this practice, the 'B' side on a number of The Drifters' records is performed by an entirely different group to that heard on the main side. Additionally, a number of singles credited to Clyde McPhatter were, in fact, made by The Drifters. When McPhatter was recording for MGM in 1959 and 1960, Atlantic released *There You Go* (2038), *Let The Boogie Woogie Roll* (2060), *Don't Dog Me* (2049) and *If I Didn't Love You* (2082) under his name. All four recordings were, however, made by The Drifters over five years earlier; *Let The Boogie Woogie Roll* even came from the same session that produced *Money Honey* in 1953! To sum up, it should be borne in mind that, apart from two different 'sets' of Drifters on either side of a record, one also finds McPhatter and The (uncredited) Drifters and McPhatter the solo artist on either side of the same single.

Left: There You Go *was made by The Drifters with Clyde McPhatter;* You Went Back On Your Word *was a McPhatter solo.*

David Baughn, who came from Harlem and whose voice bore an uncanny resemblance to McPhatter's own, was the first to replace him. New releases by The Drifters still featured McPhatter as lead singer and Baughn was deliberately chosen to enable the group to perform their current hits without disgruntling an audience used to McPhatter in lead position.[9] But his voice was beautiful, if slightly less confident than McPhatter's. On *Honey Bee* his soprano curls around a rich tapestry of vocal effects including, believe it or not, 'doo-wah doo-wah' repeated on alternate beats. The not unfamiliar plea for a girl to remain faithful is transformed into a three-minute grief-stricken wail, his voice finally spiralling upwards in a distillation of pure soul. Made at a time when a number of black vocal group records were effectively simple and poignant, *Honey Bee* was incomparable.[10] Baughn was useful for live performances where he could echo McPhatter's style, but for their records The Drifters needed a new sound, and the two tracks made with Baughn in 1955 were probably held back so that they would not compete with contemporary McPhatter sides. *Honey Bee* and *No Sweet Lovin'* were not released until 1961 and then as 'B' sides to *Some Kind Of Wonderful* and *Please Stay* respectively.

After Baughn had left, The Drifters changed personnel as often as they changed shirts. External factors including the draft and drug addiction caused many group members to leave the profession entirely. Others broke away to form groups of their own or temporarily retired, simply wishing to spend some time with their families, away from the schedule of six shows a day or three hundred miles between performances in a cramped and uncomfortable station-wagon.

Johnny Moore, born in Selma, Alabama, in 1934, joined The Drifters as David Baughn's replacement. Although he became a cornerstone of the group's success in later years he was not so fortunate during the mid-'50s. He was drafted after four sessions and did not rejoin until several years had passed and the personnel had changed completely. According to Gerhart Thrasher, his brother Andrew was fired to be replaced by Charlie Hughes, and a year later, Tommy Evans deputised for Bill Pinkney who left to form The Flyers with Bobby Hendricks. On returning to The Drifters, Pinkney brought Hendricks with him and the latter became The Drifters' sixth lead singer since the departure of Clyde McPhatter three years before.

Although their personnel has been subject to rapid and fleeting change, The Drifters are one of the few groups to have remained with the same label during their entire existence. Groups of the same name on Crown, Coral, Capitol, Class and possibly Rama have no connection with The Drifters on Atlantic; indeed, as a title, 'The Drifters' originally belonged to their manager, George Treadwell. To avoid litigation, the English Drifters became the instrumental group The Shadows. Similarly, personnel who left Treadwell's Drifters to form groups of

The Drifters in 1957. Top: *Jimmy Oliver, Charlie Hughes, Johnny Moore.* Bottom: *Tommy Evans, Gerhart Thrasher.*

their own were compelled to choose another name. Between and after periods of membership with The Drifters, bass/baritone Bill Pinkney has called his back-up group The Flyers, The Turks, The Original

Drifters (about whom more will be said in the final chapter) and The Soul Exciters. Apart from their personnel, The Drifters also changed their material, but the records released between December 1955 and August 1958 were the least successful of their entire career. Their black audience had been used to one lead singer – Clyde McPhatter – and the successful groups in the white market, within this period, were those like The Teenagers, The Coasters and The Platters whose hit records were consistently and uniformly distinctive. The Drifters used four different leads – Moore, Thrasher, Pinkney and Bobby Hendricks – and the variety of styles, albeit within a general framework of rock 'n' roll, may well have been a drawback. All were hits but comparatively minor best-sellers, unlike those made under McPhatter's leadership, and this majority did not sell well enough to make the upper reaches of the R&B chart. But in one respect the latter is no different from the national hit parade. Success in either does not always coincide with artistic quality and the recordings made by the group within this period are of greater value than their lack of popularity might suggest. Except for *Suddenly There's A Valley* the computerised ballads of Tin Pan Alley are no longer in evidence. The Drifters had turned their attentions to the white composers' rock 'n' roll tunes which were created not for the entire American population – as were Tin Pan Alley songs – but for the enjoyment of teenagers as a separate group.

Firstly, however, two songs must be mentioned which cannot be so neatly categorised. *Drifting Away From You* and *Your Promise To Be Mine* were written specially for Gerhart Thrasher by The Drifters' guitarist, Jimmy Oliver.[11] Lyrically, the familiar boy-yearns-for-girl relationship persists, but Thrasher's singing is particularly expressive. His magic carpet of a voice soars from baritone to middle C revealing at once the profound gospel heritage discussed in the first chapter. The influence of some of the great but unheralded blues shouters – Nappy Brown springs to mind – is also apparent. Gary Kramer may well have been listening to Thrasher when he wrote of the Drifters: 'Their songs are "back-breakers". They are technically difficult and couldn't even begin to be handled by the average quartet.' As the writer of the sleeve-note to the 'Rockin' 'n' Driftin'' album Kramer could afford to be generous, but he was right. The ornate patterning and ingenious rhythms of *I Gotta Get Myself A Woman* also required tremendous vocal skill. Not in the least troubled by abrupt changes in tempo, the tenor and baritone throw verses back and forth over an accompaniment which consists chiefly of drums and a finger-busting bass.

> Now when you ro-ock,
> and when you roll,
> well, well, you hypnotised me straight from head to toe.

Terry Noland and Buddy Holly's mentor Norman Petty wrote *Hypnotised* presumably after hearing Elvis Presleys' *Paralysed*. Besides a vague resemblance to the latter, it bears a tinny guitar, clipped drumming and a saxophone solo. In addition to these traditional hallmarks of rock 'n' roll, the lead singer, Johnny Moore, even attempts to roll the 'well, well' around his tongue in the manner of Presley's smouldering, animalistic delivery. The style has been likened to singing with a hot potato in the mouth. Moore could also imitate others. In comparison with McPhatter his voice was scarcely above average, but several years' experience as lead vocal with The Hawks had enabled him to gain sufficient expertise to meet all occasions.[12] *Adorable* was written by Buck Ram, the white forty-year-old manager of The Platters. As with *Soldier Of Fortune* Moore sang both in the fashion which characterised The Platters' lead singer, Tony Williams. The voice, high-pitched with an operatic richness devoid of the more emotional traits of black singing, seems no less moving for its lack of any melismatic inflection.

Black writers were not left out but they adapted to the needs of their predominantly white audience. Buddy Lucas wrote *Steamboat* for Bill Pinkney, who sings amidst an interplay from a rambling high-register pianist and saxman Sam 'The Man' Taylor, who all but blows the reed out of his instrument. *Honky Tonky*, written by underrated city bluesman Otis Blackwell is, like The Coasters' *That Is Rock 'n' Roll*, one of the few songs which attempted an explanation of the new musical idiom. The kids have gathered at a juke-joint called 'The Lemon Drop' but the juke-box stands dormant. Instead they have come to hear Joe, the local pianist:

> Now Joe's piano is out of key,
> But he still gets good harmony,
> You should hear Joe's honky tonk rock 'n' roll.

In imitation of Joe's untuned piano the narrator sings in a key unrelated to that in which the band is playing. He deliberately goes flat in order to reinforce the notion that Joe is exciting rather than technically brilliant. Joe also knows what the kids want; the showmanship of his drummer is as important as his percussive skill.

> Now Joe's got a drummer man
> With a red hot rock 'n' roll beat;
> The kids all scream, he's on the beam,
> They love the way he stomps his feet.

Bobby Hendricks and Bill Pinkney, who sang in The Flyers.

For the first time The Drifters also recorded the songs of Jerry Leiber and Mike Stoller. Jerry Wexler recalled:

One day Ahmet and I found ourselves with a very heavy schedule. We used to co-produce everything together, and I said to Ahmet or he said to me (I don't remember exactly what happened) 'Hey, the next Drifters record, let's let Leiber and Stoller do it' which was like a horrendously hair-raising notion to let somebody else do The Drifters.[13]

It was a valuable association which proved very important for The Drifters. During the period under discussion, Leiber and Stoller wrote the oft-recorded *Ruby Baby* and *Fools Fall In Love*. *Drip Drop*, a close relation to *Money Honey*, came from the same source.

Below, left to right: *Jerry Wexler, Ahmet Ertegun, Nesuhi Ertegun and Esther Phillips, with whom Clyde McPhatter recorded an unissued duet,* Heart to Heart, *for King in 1952.*
Right: *Bobby Hendricks displays his greatest influences.*

It introduced the lead voice of Bobby Hendricks, whose minimal contribution to The Drifters' recorded works is out of proportion to his talent. *Suddenly There's A Valley* and *Drip Drop* were the only songs to

emerge from The Drifters' final session in 1958. Had it been recorded ten years before, *Suddenly There's A Valley* would not have been misplaced. Swooping bass precedes an intense but clear falsetto. Pinkney and Hendricks exchange verses in a faithful re-creation of every characteristic which typified 'the sound of the birds'. From Columbus, Ohio, where he was born in 1937, Hendricks had sung with The Five Crowns and yet another 'bird' group, The Swallows. The latter recorded for After Hours and King, enjoying two Top Ten R&B hits with *Will You Be Mine* (King 4458) and *Beside You* (Federal 12329) in 1951 and 1952 respectively. Junior Denby took both tenor and baritone leads. With Eddie Rich and Dee Ernie Bailey, Hendricks sang with The Swallows 'when they were on the way down'. The Flyers' *My Only Desire* (Atco 6088), on which he also sang an emotional baritone to falsetto lead, was a slow powerful number, but it was not a hit and his ill-fortune was repeated in The Drifters. Their last session also produced *Moonlight Bay* by The Ray Ellis Singers. It was mistakenly credited to The Drifters; a bad omen that foretold imminent disarray.

Frequent bickering with George Treadwell had created a deep and irreconcilable rift. The Drifters were sacked en masse. Treadwell, whose problems included a contract, drawn up in 1954, to present The Drifters twice-yearly for ten years at The Apollo, signed a group of young New Yorkers who were appearing low on the bill at the same theatre. He changed their name from The Crowns to The Drifters. It is this group, called The Drifters, although its personnel was originally recruited from The Crowns, whose career is the subject of the rest of this book.

In January 1956 *Steamboat* and Clyde McPhatter's first solo recording, *Seven Days*, were side by side in the R&B Top Ten. Further down the list was *Adorable* together with *White Christmas* which was making its second seasonal appearance. Three years later the Drifters had no records on the chart. Why? Towards the end of the decade R&B was undergoing a major upheaval. In Detroit a young negro by the name of Berry Gordy Jr was making his first recording studio by knocking down the interior walls of his house on West Grand Boulevard; Luther Dixon was thinking how The Shirelles could be improved if he took over their production from Florence Greenburg and surrounded their voices with a back-drop of strings. More important for popular music as a whole, a white youth called Phil Spector was arranging harmonies in counterpoint on *Dontcha Worry My Little Pet*, the flip of The Teddy Bears' *To Know Him Is To Love Him* (Dore 503). Amidst these radical changes, records which featured a simple combination of group 'doo-wops', a tenor saxophone and a tinkling piano were firmly dated to the mid-'50s. The producer had come of age and soul was on the way. Future attempts to resuscitate the sound of the groups were largely unsuccessful. Rock 'n' roll was dead.

'BEAT CONCERTO' V. 'OLDIES BUT GOODIES'

During the month of August 1959 the prosaic strains of *There Goes My Baby* blared from white radio, black radio and every jukebox across the nation.

> There goes my baby
> movin' on down the line.
> Wonder where, wonder where
> wonder where she is bound?
> I broke her heart and made her cry,
> now I'm alone, so all alone.
> What can I do, what can I do?

The repetitive introductory chant, 'Bom bom, duh dud duh dud dooh, there she goes', followed by verse in which rhyme is tenuous or non-existent, creates a bald and uncompromising statement of the singer's predicament. His own foolishness has caused a precious relationship to crumble. He is hurt but not maligned. How can he make amends; what on earth can he do? He must tell the world that he needs her, wants her, loves her. Nothing else matters. It is a desperate, illogical reaction and one which he knows is ineffective.

There Goes My Baby was not only a personal expression but a product. By imposing themselves upon a talented but unsuccessful group of black singers, Jerry Leiber and Mike Stoller gave the popular music industry entirely new ideas about itself. Treadwell has insisted that he was responsible for many of the record's qualities but, whilst he helped to write it and may have encouraged Atlantic to release it, most of the ideas appear to have been primarily those of the arranger and producer. In a remarkable interview with Michael March, Leiber recently spoke about the session at which *There Goes My Baby* was made:

The session was falling apart – it was terrible. And for some reason or another I vaguely remember we had a tympani that kept going out of tune – we couldn't keep it in pitch. We were trying to create some kind of collage. We were experimenting on a date because the things that were planned for the date were falling apart. Nothing was really happening – so we started to fool around and I remember that Stan Applebaum was the arranger on the date. Mike used to do all the skeleton charts: lay out the bass line, the rhythm patterns, and those areas where different colors would appear, but he would often not write the actual string line or the reed line, though the main structure would be there. And Stanley wrote something that sounded like some Caucasian take-off and we had this Latin beat going on this out of tune tympani and The Drifters were singing something in another key, but the total effect – there was something magnetic about it. And the date was considered a fiasco. I mean everybody thought it was just a waste, a terrible waste of time and money. And we took the playbacks to Atlantic one afternoon to play them for Ahmet and Jerry and we were playing the tapes back and we were all grieving and we were saying 'oh, there's nothing salvagable about this' – and then we played this one side and I said and Mike said 'there's something fascinating about it – you know it's a fucking mess. But there's something very magnetic about it.' And Jerry Wexler was eating his lunch on his desk and he said 'Man, get the fuck out of here with that.' You know – 'get out of here with that – I hate it', you know – 'It's out of tune and it's phony and it's shit and get it out of here!' – but we kept on insisting there was something and Ahmet was listening too and he kept saying 'You know, I think . . . well maybe we ought to, you know, try and put it out.' And they put it out and it became number one in the country. And I'd be listening to the radio sometimes and hear it and I was convinced it sounded like two stations playing one thing.[1]

Leiber may have meant to say that it sounded like one station playing two different records, for the effects were multi-dimensional. In Britain, Frankie Lymon had been allowed to record with a full string orchestra, in 1957, and was to some extent a star. In the United States he was a precocious black kid who got rich quick by hanging around street corners. 'You can't use strings with those guys' had been the unspoken cry,[2] but the strings on *There Goes My Baby* were not the dull, weepy violins used on popular recordings by white singers for the past twenty years. They rose and fell with a stark, *triste* and positive allegiance to classical music. With justification the song might have been called *There Goes Tchaikovsky*. Kettle-drums pounded throughout, but more obviously during the deeper, quieter moments of the string passages, strengthening a resemblance to the 1812 Overture. It is an interesting coincidence that, like the works of the Russian composer, *There Goes My Baby* can also be described as 'notable for a vivid, forceful scoring and for an often expressed melancholy.'[3] Ben E King sang in a higher key than his normal baritone range. The effect was two-fold: it heightened the coarse, untrained, root-gospel quality of his voice and imparted an air of hopelessness to the theme of the song.

The eclectic combination of such widely differing styles had previously worked for George Gershwin, whose piano preludes and other concert works had been largely inspired by the stylistic characteristics of black religious music, but The Drifters had made an unprecedented switch in reverse. The introduction of the violin to rhythm and blues unleashed a trend as significant in popular music as the invention of the electric guitar. Others soon adapted the works of major classical composers.

Jackie Wilson was one of the many vocalists who continued to pay close attention to The Drifters long after his idol, Clyde McPhatter, had left them. Besides *Alone At Last* (Brunswick 55170), an adaptation of Tchaikovsky's Piano Concerto in B Flat Minor, Wilson also had *My Empty Arms* (55201), a pop version of Ruggiero Leoncavallo's 'On With The Motley' from 'I Pagliacci' and a million-selling record with Camille Saint-Saëns' 'My Heart At Thy Sweet Voice' from 'Samson and Delilah' under the new title of *Night* (55166). For some, the realisation that one could use strings with black singers meant that urban R&B lost a number of its more sophisticated performers. Down in Texas, Eddie Silvers began to supervise violins behind Bobby Bland. Those in charge of white rock 'n' rollers were also quick to see the possibilities. Stringed instruments, played pizzicato, were soon heard on the last records of Buddy Holly.

The musical press called the new sound 'Beat Concerto', but George Treadwell explained it in simpler terms: 'We experimented with the sound we introduced until we found exactly what we wanted. We use strings and a guitar with a rock 'n' roll beat to back it and carry the voices of the quartet on top. It's a heck of a sound.' Treadwell can be forgiven for his immodesty. A good R&B hit will sell 350,000 copies. An exceptionally fortunate R&B hit will sell 500,000 and still be bought by blacks only. To achieve sales in excess of that figure a record has to be bought by both races. *There Goes My Baby* was instrumental in bringing The Drifters from the comparative obscurity of the large but segregated black community into popularity in over half-a-million white homes. For an experienced but inglorious group, The Crowns had it made. They bowed daily in the direction of The Atlantic Record Corporation for ever more.

Previously known as The Five Crowns, the group were originally managed by Lover Patterson who appears, with George Treadwell, as

The Five Crowns including, at the far right, 'Doc' Green.

composer in the credits to *There Goes My Baby*. Patterson died in 1965. Had he lived he might well have been able to clarify the confusion which surrounds the personnel changes of the group. James Clark, Doc Green, John Clark, Claud 'Little Nickie' Clark and lead vocalist, Wilber Paul, were amongst the first personnel. They made numerous singles for Rainbow to which they were signed on 29 August 1952, pre-dating McPhatter and his Drifters, who did not record together until a year later. Other releases on Old Town, Gee and Trans-world followed. All are highly valued by group collectors but none set the world on fire at its time of issue. Claud Clark joined the comparatively successful Harptones in 1954 and the rest of the group were not immune from the rapid changes that beset most of their contemporaries. In March 1958 they shortened their name to The Crowns and released *I'll Kiss And Make Up* (R&B 6901). The record featured Ben E King (lead), Charles Thomas (tenor), Doc Green (baritone) and Ellsbury Hobbs (bass). Atlantic were responsible for the distribution of the small R&B label and had no qualms about releasing the same group's future records under the name of The Drifters.

Unlike many narcissistic white artists, most black artists are rarely preoccupied with the details of their careers. Gentle enquiries into the past frequently elicit: 'What do you want to know about them for? They're nothin' records man.' Ben E King told one interviewer[4] that

Lover Patterson sang lead on the Rainbow issues whilst he himself sang on the records for Gee and Caravan. When interviewed five years later he had changed his mind. The Gee and Caravan issues were 'before my time'.[5] Whatever the truth, The Five Crowns made eleven records between October 1952 and March 1958. On their fast numbers, *$19.50 Bus, I Don't Have To Hurt No More* (Rainbow) and *Oo-Wee Baby* (Riviera), there was often a clear distinction between voices and the instrumental accompaniment, which included a meandering piano, guitars and a hot tenor break. Similarly, the slow sides – on which Paul's emotional, wavering and professionally slurred voice was heard to better effect – still had an accompaniment from a small band of accomplished musicians who made their presence felt. Apart from the discordant and mediocre *God Bless You* (Gee), all their records were good group sounds. Some, including the standard *Keep It A Secret* (Rainbow) and *You Came To Me* (Riviera), which had a harmonic introduction, a spoken verse and a falsetto lead, were very beautiful indeed. Nevertheless, The Five Crowns were not dissimilar from hundreds of other fine quartets. It is little short of incredible that the same group – barring unimportant changes of personnel – should have produced *There Goes My Baby*. Why had the sound changed so suddenly and so dramatically?

Groups, which depended upon the sales of 45 rpm records to ensure a decent livelihood like most performers of popular music, had to respond to the likes and dislikes of their audience. They were conscious of the need to keep pace with public taste. While the dominant audience was middle-aged, popular music remained relatively unchanged for twenty years. Now the industry felt compelled to ring the changes in order to satisfy an adolescent audience, whose rapidly changing tastes paralleled natural stages in their maturing. But groups did not control their own sounds and destinies; the decisions were invariably taken by older, wiser men. Who decided to put oboes behind The Cardinals, an orchestra behind The Orioles, a saxophone solo in records by The Coasters, or violins and kettle drums behind The Drifters? In all cases, the producers made the decisions for the groups. In the last two examples, the producers were Jerry Leiber and Mike Stoller.

Perhaps the most renowned composers to have emerged from the rock 'n' roll era, Leiber and Stoller first collaborated in 1950 when small independent R&B labels on the west coast were enjoying unprecedented sales. Leiber recalled:

Our first records were such items as *Corn Whiskey* by Amos Milburn on Aladdin [probably *Good Good Whiskey* (Aladdin 3218)], *Hard Times* by Charles Brown (Aladdin 3116), *That's What The Good Book Says* by The Robins (Modern 807). It was a transition period... white youngsters were digging the root blues and dancing to this exciting music.[6]

Their predilection for the folk roots of American music is explained by their early environment. Said Leiber: 'I was brought up in Baltimore... in a black and white neighbourhood and all I heard as a youngster were blues and country music.' In 1956, Atlantic purchased the entire collection of tapes and masters owned by the Los Angeles-based Spark label. Amongst the finds were some exceptionally good R&B group records including *Riot In Cell Block No 9* (Spark 103) and *Framed* (Spark 107) by The Robins. Both had been written and produced by Leiber and Stoller. The Robins became The Coasters on Atco[7] – Atlantic's subsidiary label – and Leiber and Stoller went with them. A non-exclusive production agreement was signed and the couple produced material, which for the most part they had also written, for other Atlantic artists, including Ruth Brown, Joe Turner, Lavern Baker and The Drifters.

The immediate follow-ups to *There Goes My Baby* had no classical connotations, but the violins were retained and the percussion featured a subtle raft of Latin American rhythms. Of Brazilian rhythms Leiber recalled in *Billboard*, 12 July 1969: 'This was an influence we had felt in California, where the rhythm of the samba had much impact.' First heard in *Dance With Me* and *This Magic Moment*, a shuffling Latin beat became a distinctive characteristic of many later releases.

The Robins were the first group to work with Leiber and Stoller.

Rhythm 'N Blues SLEEPER OF THE WEEK

"LOOP DE LOOP MAMBO" (2:40)
[Quintet BMI—Leiber, Stoller]

"FRAMED" (2:45)
[Quintet BMI—Leiber, Stoller]

THE ROBINS

(Spark 107)

● The Robins come up with what looks like a winner in "Loop De Loop Mambo." The group really rides this one with a spectacular treatment of a solid piece of material. The lads get in on the current dance craze with an item that has a freshness, drive and novelty. Should be the best the Robins have come up with yet. The flip, "Framed," is another humorous jump item, in which the group uses the familiar narration and song technique. Lyrics are just what the title implies. The hero is framed by the police. Cute ditty. Two good sides, but "Loop De Loop Mambo" should make it quick.

Ben E King sang lead vocal on only 11 of The Drifters 124 tracks, but of all their personnel he is the best known, particularly in Britain, where he has toured on numerous occasions as a solo artist. Born Benjamin Earl Nelson in Henderson, North Carolina, on 28 September 1938, he moved to New York with his family at the age of nine. In order to assist his father, who had established a small restaurant business, King was forced to leave Seward Park High School before graduation. At the age of six he performed in his local church choir and he continued to sing on the steps of old brownstone houses in the poorer suburbs of New York City with many informal quartets: 'All I'd have to see was three or four guys in the neighborhood standing on the corner harmonising one of the popular songs and I'd join right in.' Lover Patterson heard him singing to the diners in his father's luncheonette and asked him to join The Five Crowns in 1956. Whilst his name was an addition to the composer credits of *There Goes My Baby*, King did not write music. Like Frankie Lymon he 'didn't know nothin' about music – written-down music that is.' George Goldner and Joe Kilsky arranged for the sheet music for Lymon's hits to be written down by a professional arranger after their records were made. King employed a similar method:

I'd sit down with this old guitar I have that's missing all but three strings – no-one else could possibly play it, but I pick out tunes and, when I have something, I'll play it for someone who can write it.

Both *Save The Last Dance For Me* and *I Count The Tears* (written by Doc Pomus and Mort Shuman) were recorded with King singing lead vocal but released after he had embarked on a solo career. *Save The Last Dance For Me* introduced The Drifters to an international audience. It is clear, in retrospect, that it also introduced Phil Spector. As far as The Drifters' admirers knew, Leiber and Stoller were the master-minds behind all their releases. Today, albums compiled from recordings of the period bear the magic words – 'A Leiber-Stoller Production'. But listening now to *Save The Last Dance For Me*, it is inconceivable that Spector was not in the studio when it was recorded. The June 1970 *Fusion* interview with Wexler included his version of the Spector story:

They [Leiber and Stoller] found him at the same high school that they had been at . . . in Hollywood. Lester Sill had been in business with them with Spark records. He found Phil and sent him here, and Leiber and Stoller sort of watched over him.

Phil was very young. And he came to work for us, doing A and R work. I don't think he stayed for a full year and he went out as an independent. And I think the first big hit he cut was *Corinna Corinna* with Ray Peterson. And the rest of course was, you know, fantastic . . . He is

Ben E King in action.

a person who presides over studio happenings. He confects it, he gets it together, in the studio. I don't think there's been an artist that Phil Spector has ever developed that has ability worth a damn. You don't even think of them as mainstream artists . . . he was a Pygmalion, I mean he took raw clay, and fabricated it and molded it and breathed on it and it came to life. Now that is what you might call a producer's producer.

Born in the Bronx on 26 December 1940, Spector was not bound by the conventions which had inhibited older producers. The arsenal of dazzling production and engineering ideas he was later to put to good use behind The Crystals and The Ronettes, germinated during his contract with Atlantic. He mixed voices, double-tracked, dubbed on extra instruments and used almost anything including five drum sets or chains attached to the piano. Spector's now familiar 'wall of sound' was born. The musical press had to drop 'beat concerto' and 'rock-a-beguine'. *Save The Last Dance*, we were told, was 'wind-tunnel rock'! Although he is said to have played guitar for *On Broadway*, Spector's influence is not apparent after *Save The Last Dance For Me*. It is clear that he expressed a preference for working with Ben E King on his own.

Legend would have it that, early in 1960, King braved a raging blizzard to fight his way to Atlantic's recording studios for another session

with The Drifters. The other members failed to arrive and with Phil Spector conveniently at hand with *Spanish Harlem* – a song he had written with Jerry Leiber – Atlantic decided not to waste the opportunity. Romantic but incorrect. King was certainly destined to become a solo artist, but before *Spanish Harlem* (Atco 6185) he had already cut *Brace Yourself* (Atco 6166), an Otis Blackwell number, and *How Often* (Atlantic 2067) a duet with Lavern Baker. He followed these with a string of highly successful records, but they were invariably bogged down with the strictly commercial, heavy and uninteresting arrangements of Stanley Applebaum and Klaus Ogermann. There was a brief period in 1964 when he made two records, *It's All Over* (Atco 6315) and *Seven Letters* (Atco 6328), which rivalled Solomon Burke in the convincing display of emotional involvement. But King lost the abrasive quality that originally made his voice so exciting. Of *Rough Edges* – his latest album – Ed Ochs remarked: 'It has none.'[8]

Before King's departure, Johnny Lee Williams took a solitary lead vocal on *True Love, True Love*. The tune, the sentiment and Williams' pleasing but undistinguished tenor were all too pretty to be called R&B. Yet the record sold inexplicably well in the black market. The top side, *Dance With Me*, was a big hit in both racial markets but would not have achieved a million sales without the success of *True Love, True Love*. Williams came and went quietly. A record by Johnny Lee Williams out of Memphis in June 1962 (*Nona Baby/Teach Me How*: Louis 6801) might be a clue to his later activities, but the label was owned by ex-Presley bass player Bill Black and the connection is somewhat slender.[9]

Although the change from 'beat concerto' through 'rock-a-beguine' to 'wind-tunnel rock' had been achieved within the space of five smash hits, a vague smattering of each style remained with The Drifters for the next decade. To achieve lasting success in the white market, with all its opportunities for wealth, was now the main aim. As far as Atlantic's producers were concerned, it was not possible to achieve such fame upon the vocal talents of a black group in isolation. Their records required an extra sophistication. To reach the white market and remain successful in it necessitated surrounding black groups with the customary trappings of the popular white singer. Harmony was sacrificed as a chorus of chanting girls, elaborate percussion, a string orchestra and a heavenly choir became the norm. For the casual listener, it became increasingly difficult to distinguish a record made by a group from one made by a solo performer. Apart from the lead singer, the remainder of the group were now content to mouth an unobtrusive drift of stereotyped 'oohs' and 'aahs'. There was little point in doing anything else for, very soon, even this small contribution was drowned amidst a welter of instrumental combinations. Moreover, a female chorus (in the case of The Drifters, one which included Dionne Warwick, Dee Dee Warwick and Doris Troy) allowed no room for the exquisite harmony for which black groups had previously been noted. Nor could such a back-drop compensate for its loss. The Warwick sisters were blessed with technically superb voices and, like Doris Troy, each proved to be a successful solo performer. But, singing in unison behind The Drifters, their massed pseudo-gospel chants became an unnecessary irritation.

Having returned The Drifters to immense popularity, their producers were content to repeat the same formula over and over again. Apart from *Baltimore* and *Hey Senorita* (a throw-back sound written by Lover Patterson and recorded under the original title of *Dum De Dum Dum* by The Cadillacs in 1957) The Drifters rarely recorded without a string section again. When Ben E King left Atlantic in 1970, it is pertinent to record that he explained that his departure was due to the fact that every producer with whom he worked wanted him to deliver a copy of *Spanish Harlem* or *Stand By Me*, his initial solo hits. Ertegun, Wexler and Dowd were previously important in arranging and recording the voices of the singers. They had permitted – even encouraged – McPhatter to be himself and to treat each new song on his own personal terms. It is one of the numerous reasons why his work survives repeated listening, and why more recent Drifters recordings demand less consideration.

In keeping with the deliberate softening inflicted upon rock 'n' roll in general, The Drifters' lead singers became less intense, less neurotic and decidedly mellow. One would not have guessed that Rudy Lewis, who replaced Ben E King in 1960, was one of two male vocalists to

The Drifters in 1959. Top: *Johnny Lee Williams and Charles Thomas;* bottom: *Ellsbury Hobbs and Doc Green.*

perform with The Clara Ward Singers. His voice was rich and sweet but he rarely sang more than one note per syllable, and was not allowed to show any flair for syncopation. Perhaps because his gospel origins were the least noticeable of any of the group's front vocalists, the records upon which he sang were sensationally popular. Of the period, Nik Cohn remarked, 'no matter how many individuals came or went, they always kept the same basic sound, tight and immensely commercial.'[10] It is precisely because The Drifters' sound remained constant that many of their personnel changes made little constructive contribution. During Lewis' residence as lead, Tommy Evans returned from The Ravens to replace bass, Ellsbury Hobbs, who was drafted. It was Evans' second period of duty with The Drifters, but he left again to be replaced by

Johnny Terry who, like Clyde McPhatter and Evans, had also sung with Billy Ward's Dominoes. On leaving the armed services, Johnny Moore had tried to establish himself as a solo artist, recording for Melic and Sue under the pseudonym of Johnny Darrow. Apart from *Don't Start Me Talking* (Sue 728) his attempts were entirely unsuccessful and he returned to The Drifters in 1963 taking the lead from Rudy Lewis when it suited him. Doc Green also split to re-form The Moonglows with Alexander Graves, but their work for Lana, Crimson and Times Square were chiefly re-recordings of The Moonglows biggest hits and too archaic for mass acceptance in revived form. Green was replaced by Eugene Pearson, whose career illustrates the unfortunate rut into which black vocal groups, especially The Drifters, had fallen.

Pearson began his professional career with The Embers, and wrote *Paradise Hill* (Herald 410), their small hit late in 1953. After leaving

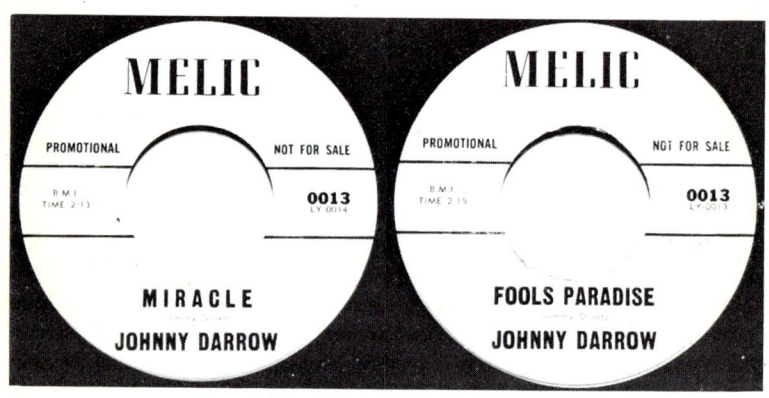

Johnny Moore recorded under the name of Johnny Darrow.

The Embers, he performed the same service for another quartet, The Rivileers, who recorded for Baton, owned by the Sol Rabinowitz mentioned earlier. With The Rivileers, Pearson sang tenor and wrote much of their material including their biggest hit of 1954 *A Thousand Stars* (Baton 200). By 1958 he had joined The Cleftones. Their lead singer, Herbie Cox, was recently interviewed. In the precise language that befits his current occupation as a computer programmer, he recalled:

All the fellows are the original fellows. By name Berman Patterson, Charles James, Warren Corbin. Gene Pearson technically may not be considered an original, he joined the group two years after we started.[11]

The Cleftones, including Pearson, came from New York, where they had attended Jamaica High School together. Their big hits of 1956 included *You Baby You* (Gee 1000) and *This Little Girl Of Mine* (Gee 1011). Returning from the limbo to which many black groups were consigned after the initial impetus of rock 'n' roll, The Cleftones were fortunate to notch up three hits in 1961. For these – *Heart And Soul* (Gee 1064), *For Sentimental Reasons* (Gee 1067) and *Lover Come Back To Me* (Gee 1079) – Pearson sang second tenor and usually wrote the flip-side. When The Drifters toured Britain during 1965 the reason for their continued existence as a group was immediately apparent. Terry and Pearson were not there to sing; their sole function was to dance at live performances. But it was not their fault. The audience required little more than the lead voice that they had been accustomed to from the groups' recordings. Harmony was expendable in a recording

THE RIVILEERS
(Baton 205)

B+ "ETERNAL LOVE" (2:43) [Challenge BMI — Pearson] A soft and downy ballad waxed prettily by the smooth working group. Romantic lyrics that should appeal to the starry eyed. Dreamy wax. Should pull good sales.

B "CAROLYN" (2:40) [Challenge BMI—Delaney] A slow rhythmic ditty, also of a romantic nature, dished up in the soft smooth style of the Rivileers. Good deck, but outmatched by "Eternal Love."

Gene Pearson sang with The Rivileers and wrote their biggest hits including Eternal Love.

studio; it was considered even more unnecessary on stage. Tired of his role as dancing stooge, writing nothing and scarcely opening his mouth, Pearson left The Drifters and took a manual job for the next five years. When The Cleftones came out of retirement for a number of revivalist rock 'n' roll shows in 1970 Pearson was with them singing his heart out.

If group singing, or lack of it, was no longer important to the audience there has to be another explanation for the remarkable trail of hits sung by Rudy Lewis. *Some Kind Of Wonderful*, *Please Stay*, *When My Little Girl Is Smiling*, *Sweets For My Sweet* and *On Broadway* were enormously successful, while *Up On The Roof* gave The Drifters their fourth gold disc. Charlie Gillett has written 'some sound too lush and sweet to stand much attention now' [12] and although I am tempted to dismiss them as lightly, he was reviewing an album and could afford to be brief. The key to their popularity and, paradoxically, the root of the problem, is to be found on the back of those Drifters' albums which

SLEEPER OF THE WEEK

"CAN'T SEEM TO LAUGH ANYMORE" (2:57)
"NEVER AGAIN" (2:06)

JOHNNY PARKER
(Capitol 1162)

JOHNNY PARKER

● Disk star Johnny Parker bows into the wax horizon in a blaze of glory with a side that's bound to step out and prove to be a heavy winner for music operators. That music ops will have to keep their eyes peeled for Parker is easily seen in the top deck, "Can't Seem To Laugh Anymore." The tune itself is a cinch to clinch with music ops and fans—add Parker's vocal rendition, and you've got a smash hit on your hands. Ditty is a slowly woven tender item—the kind that makes you keep singing, humming and whistling the infectious melody. It's a plush romantic effort, well loaded with sentimentality from the word go. Choral background, matched with some excellent orchestral patter via maestro Pete Rugulo all blend to make the disk a top notch performance. Johnny shows his versatile vocal style on the flip, by coming up with a rhythm number that should do fairly well. The side we're ga-ga about is the top one—ops should grab it!

Songwriters for Clyde McPhatter and The Drifters; top: *Carole King, Ellie Greenwich and Clyde Otis;* bottom: *Johnny Parker and Van McCoy.*

contain their biggest hits. For one such sleeve-note, Bob Altshuler wrote: 'Publishers scramble to get their best numbers recorded by The Drifters.' For another sleeve he continued: 'An indication of the stature The Drifters enjoy can be gathered from the persistent attention they receive from Tin Pan Alley. The Drifters are eagerly sought after by song-writers and publishers, hoping the group will record their latest efforts.' Thus The Drifters came to record songs from the top pop composers of the day. Wexler described the system in the *Fusion* interview:

... there was one little group that worked together, New York people even though part was transplanted to California. Spector worked with

Jeff Barry and Ellie Greenwich, he worked with Barry Mann and Cynthia, he worked with Carol King and Gerry Goffin, he worked with Leiber and Stoller. It was a circular thing. They wrote the songs and they produced and we used their material and they made records for us and Spector co-wrote with them. It was really a closed shop.

Like Burt Bacharach and Bob Hilliard, who also broke into the 'closed shop', the writers Wexler mentions have been described as great modern composers, but, apart from Spector and Leiber and Stoller, they are also overrated. Goffin and King, like Barry Mann and Cynthia Weil, were a husband and wife team. Their trademarks – a string orchestration; a slow, often spoken introduction; the splitting of the third line of a verse into two rhyming parts and a penchant for the words 'little girl' – rarely inspired black singers. They made a lot of pop-cum-R&B for girl singers including The Cookies, Little Eva and her sister, Idalia Boyd, Freda Payne, The Chiffons and The Shirelles, who recorded *Will You Love Me Tomorrow*, perhaps Goffin and King's most memorable achievement. Another notable hit was Freddie Scott's *Hey Girl*. They also turned out hits for Gene Pitney, Steve Lawrence, Tony Orlando, James Darren and particularly Bobby Vee, for whom they provided many successful numbers. All were published by Aldon Music owned by Al Nevins and Don Kirshner who, more recently, has been partly responsible for the success of The Monkees and The Archies.

Weil and Mann; Goffin and King; Bacharach and Hilliard. They were interchangeable, and very much alike. Their songs were sometimes thoughtful but more often corny and self-conscious; they possessed ingenious rhythmic structure or fade-out endings; new complexities of verse or back in 'the land of make believe'. All white men and women; all writing for 'The Public' and all in it for the money. In the light of Altshuler's assertions one can understand why The Drifters added this blatantly commercial, 'Teen Pan Alley' pop to their repertoire. Fortunately, as he pointed out, they were the best songs each composer had to offer. We must be grateful that Bacharach gave *The Story Of My Life* to Marty Robbins; *Magic Moments* to Perry Como and *Me Japanese Boy* to Bobby Goldsborough. But the situation was not so much the fault of the song-writers as of the producers. In a recent interview with Grace Lichtenstein, Carole King explained why concern for 'the public' dominated their songs: 'If you wanted to be a rock 'n' roll song-writer in 1961, you joined what amounted to a musical chicken coop as a contract writer.' Carole and Jerry Goffin, barely a year out of high school, signed contracts with producer Donny Kirshner, who later became known as the king of the 'bubblegum' music. Every day they and the other contract writing teams would come to work at 1650 Broadway.

We each had a little cubbyhole with just enough room for a piano, a bench and maybe a chair for the lyricist – if you were lucky. You'd sit there and write and you could hear someone in the next cubby hole composing some song exactly like yours. The pressure, the Brill Building atmosphere was really terrific, because Donny would play one song-writer against another. He'd say, 'We need a latest smash hit,' and we'd all go back and write a song and the next day we'd each audition for Bobby Vee's producer. *Take Good Care Of My Baby*, one of our biggest hits, came about that way.

The system did not exactly foster inventiveness. We all wrote interchangeably, Neil Sedaka, Howard Greenfield, Cynthia Weil and Barry Mann, Gerry and me.

Bacharach frequently took three months to produce any one of his songs. After going over the lyrics some 400 times, he would take plans of the choral background through numerous other stages and thoroughly rehearse the chosen singer's performance. By the time he had remixed the play-backs and inspected the pressing plant to choose a perfect test pressing, the finished article bore no trace of the earthy spontaneity achieved by Ahmet Ertegun when he wrote *Whatcha Gonna Do*. Bacharach's preoccupation with clinical perfection is apparent in recordings of his songs by other black singers including Chuck Jackson and Jerry Butler, but their robust voices and their experience in a variety of R&B styles – Jackson with The Del-Vikings and Butler with The Impressions – enabled them to infuse his often pallid material with the appropriate emotion, optimism, anxiety or despair. If Perry Como had recorded *Any Day Now* (Chuck Jackson, Wand 122) or *Make It Easy On Yourself* (Jerry Butler, Veejay 451) the results would not have appealed to those who require a degree of involvement or conviction in the performer's voice.

I have not heard recordings of Rudy Lewis with The Clara Ward Singers, but it is not unreasonable to assume that his voice lost the black gospel inflection he thought inappropriate to the straight pop compositions he was required to sing with The Drifters. When Dionne Warwick sang Bacharach she became a 'musicians' singer', a sophisticated artist far removed from the earlier ragged but exciting role she had performed with a gospel ensemble, The Drinkard Singers. The voice of Rudy Lewis may have been anaesthetised in a similar manner. Whatever the explanation, neither audience nor industry had yet fully embraced the sweaty, hysterical tide of soul music and the combination of cliché-ridden songs and a mellow, inoffensive lead voice enabled The Drifters to continue their staggering succession of hit records.

It is no coincidence that, in this period, the majority of numbers which stood out above the level of the general love-song were written, if not by Leiber and Stoller, by black writers. Otis Blackwell wrote the extremely Coasterish *I Feel Good All Over* and Rudy Clark penned

The Drifters in 1965. Top: *Gene Pearson, Charles Thomas, Johnny Moore.* Bottom: *Gene Pearson, Johnny Moore, Johnny Terry, Charles Thomas.*

Didn't It. Leiber and Stoller contributed a song which was reminiscent of their first collaborations more than ten years before. The second and third verses to *If You Don't Come Back* illustrate the humour, guts and well-observed narrative that are persistently absent from the songs of Bacharach or Goffin and King.

> I threw myself up against the wall now,
> I tore my clothes and I sobbed;
> I ran out in the street
> In my stockinged feet,
> Yelling 'Police, I been robbed'.

> Mrs Brown been talking about me
> To the people way across the street.
> She said 'I cooked that boy now a bucket of stew,
> But the poor thing just won't eat'.

The lyric is punctuated with menacing low key brass riffs and Johnny Moore sings as if he were about to lose his sanity. Everything about the disc was too bluesy for Rudy Lewis' less forceful voice, but, oddly, he took the lead on the top-side, *Rat Race*. Written by 'black-jack of all trades' Van McCoy, as well as Leiber and Stoller, it was the toughest of The Drifters' excursions into the realm of the socio-pop song. Two others, *Up On The Roof* and *Mexican Divorce* – described by Rolontz as a 'critical and emotional slap at quickie divorces'[13] – also explored the theme of man and his behaviour. Although these less than revolutionary critiques of the tensions of American life can scarcely have inspired Country Joe and The Fish, it was one of the first occasions when popular songs concerned more serious issues than a boy who just had to have a girl. Perhaps they looked forward to the day when popular music became the artistic language of the rock generation. Fortunately, for those with less progressive (or philistine) musical tastes some people were still 'doo-wopping'.

The early '60s are generally held to mark the death of group R&B, but the period was almost as interesting as the years during which such sounds and styles were created. In 1959 and 1960, 16 and 18 different vocal groups had best-selling records in the national Top Twenty. 1961 was, however, their most profitable year since the full scale promotion of rock 'n' roll in 1956. Over 35 groups of all creeds and colours achieved similar success. Most belonged to an underrated and documentarily neglected musical school. According to an American observer who had analysed 'Billboard's Hot Hundred', such groups were a collection of impoverished college kids anxious to earn pin money in order to finance their studies, but this view was only partly true. They may have been impoverished, but only a small proportion were still students and there

The Drifters. Top: *Billy Davis, Gene Pearson, Charles Thomas, Johnny Moore, Johnny Terry.* Bottom: *Gene Pearson, Johnny Terry, Charles Thomas, Johnny Moore, Billy Davis.*

were other factors by which they could be more readily distinguished.

Racial origin, for example, was not evident from their music. They were black, Puerto Rican, Mexican, Anglo-Saxon or Italian youths from the Carnesie section of Brooklyn. For once it didn't matter. Their appreciation for older forms of R&B was a cohesive agent. All, with varying degrees of success, emulated the harmony of negro groups with whom they had had considerable empathy as youngsters only seven or eight years before. The white adolescents were just plain 'hip', but the others came from minority immigrant groups. Racial intolerance was a situation that Puerto Ricans, Mexicans and, to a lesser extent, those of Italian extraction, shared with the black man, although I do not advance it as a reason for their inclination towards his music. If they did not record the standards so beloved by early black groups, they invented their own inane, nonsensical ditties with the same harmonising aim in mind. Naturally, some like The Lettermen or The Castells became too lush and smooth in their desire for universal appeal, but the majority remained in rapport with the tastes of their own age group.

The Capris produced *There's A Moon Out Tonight* (Planet 1011) which had actually been made in 1958; The Echoes had *Baby Blue* (Segway 1003) and The Dovells sang *Bristol Stomp* (Parkway 827). Other big hits came from The Chimes, The Belmonts, and The Demensions. Cathy Jean and The Roomates and The Marcels were both integrated groups. Although they were not the first (The Del-Vikings and later The Crests were pioneers in that respect) The Marcels' combination of two white and three black singers bears testimony to the racial solidarity which music can create. The Pittsburgh group gave a new lease of life to Rodgers and Hart's *Blue Moon* (Colpix 186). The goofy 'bom ba ba bom' introduction was effective in restoring to respectability the bass singer who, since the mid-'50s, had been much neglected. The Regents, The Devotions, The Edsels and many more enjoyed best-selling records with nursery-like rhymes all of whose primary appeal lay in the sharp contrast between a beautiful, resonant bass introduction and a high tenor lead. This re-worked if not entirely revitalised return to the roots was more genuine than many later so-called rock 'n' roll revivals. Amongst other groups whose surnames implied an Italian or Spanish ancestry were The Duprees. They rose to fame with *You Belong To Me* (Coed 569) which The Orioles had made in November 1952. Similarly, *What Are You Doing New Year's Eve* and *Till Then*, made by The Orioles in 1949 and 1953, were revived by Dante and The Evergreens (Madison 143) and The Classics (Musicnote 1116) respectively. Over eight years after it was written, white group Kathy Young and The Innocents took Gene Pearson's song *A Thousand Stars* (Indigo 108) high into the Top Twenty. Gladys Knight and The Pips had similar success with *Every Beat Of My Heart* (Fury 1050), a song Johnny Otis had written for The Royals in 1952. Albums

The Del Vikings – one of the first integrated R&B groups.

by The Marcels, The Regents and The Dovells featured, in entirety, songs made popular by, amongst others, The Teenagers, The Eldorados, The Spaniels and The Five Satins between six and ten years before. The sleeve of The Dovells' album (Parkway 7010) made it clear that each group member had chosen to perform a couple of his all-time favourite group recordings. Significantly, 11 of the 12 songs had previously been popularised by black vocal groups.

Soul, in the shape of The Jarmels, The Miracles or The Marvelettes, was still struggling to establish itself. The other big hits by black groups owed an enormous debt to their predecessors whose harmony had captivated the white audience during the early '50s. The G-Clefs scored with *I Understand* (Terrace 7500), a tune which blended *Auld Lang Syne* into its arrangement. Exactly the same formula was successful for The Four Tunes in 1954. The G-Clefs were originally popular with *Ka-Ding-Dong* (Pilgrim 715) but had resumed their education before recording *I Understand* in 1961. Other groups who had spent years in obscurity were now back on the best-selling charts. In addition to The Cleftones, Maurice Williams and The Zodiacs[14] (*Stay*, Herald 552), The Chantels (*Look In My Eyes*, Carlton 555) and Shep and The Limelites (*Daddy's Home*, Hull 740) were extremely successful. New black groups, including The Jive Five and The Dreamlovers also sang in styles that were faithful to those of an earlier period. Their big hits, *My True Story* (Beltone 1006) and *When We Get Married* (Heritage 102), were both romantic teenage delights delivered at a snail's pace and characterised by the use of unobtrusive harmony and falsetto wailing. White solo performers Johnny Maestro (ex-lead of The Crests) and Curtis Lee and black singer Gene Chandler also enjoyed hit recordings sounding essentially the same in style as the songs featured by the groups of the same period.

A black group, Little Caesar and The Romans, summed it all up with *Those Oldies But Goodies* (Delfi 4158), a Top Ten hit in June 1961. A less successful cover version by an Italian group, Nino and The Ebbtides (Madison 162) was even better. Both contained snatches of harmonic refrains from former black group hits. Despite racial differences – and the gap in years – such groups were not only musically compatible with those they idolised. When asked how his group got together, Tony Armato of The Passions replied: 'In the back of a movie house. In the alley-way. From there we went across the street to the pool-room, Kelley's Pool-room. We were all together, nine or ten guys. We split up, half of us became The Passions; half of us became The Mystics.'[15]

Nino & The Ebb-Tides

After sharing some of the hit loot on "Those Oldies But Goodies," Nino & The Ebb-Tides have come back with "Juke Box Saturday Night," a teen-beat version of the years-ago Modernaires hit, which shows promise of being a big one for them. It broke on the Top 100 this week in the #99 slot.

The group is comprised of four young boys from the east Bronx section of New York City. Nino, 21, sings lead tenor; Vinny, 22, sings baritone and bass; Tony, 22, is second tenor, and Slim, 21, is also a tenor and sometimes sings lead. Nino and Vinny grew up together, joined forces with the other two in 1959, and began developing a group style. A chance meeting with Madison Records prexy Larry Utal led to an audition and then a contract.

All four boys are members of the U. S. Naval Reserve and train together at Fort Schuyler, N. Y.

Nino and The Ebbtides covered Little Caesar and The Romans' Those Oldies but Goodies. *From* Cashbox, *1961*.

The Passions made *Just To Be With You* (Audicon 102) and four more singles which did nothing at all. Like their black counterparts a decade before, their talent was used up in one brief, bright, burst of

The Heartbeats with James (Shep) Sheppard.

glory. Perhaps they were written off as somebody's tax loss. Whatever it was, none of the groups mentioned within the last few pages was any more durable than the black groups of 1956 or 1957, but there was a crucial difference. The Anglo-Saxons or Italians often benefited from the advantages of a superior education. Tony Armato could take up architectural plumbing, whilst his friendly rivals The Mystics are now in the engineering field. For blacks it was mostly a different story. Claude Johnson, one half of the duo Don and Juan, told of his troubles in the recording industry and why he preferred to keep on singing even if he was reduced to standing on the corner where passers-by could drop coins into a tin cup:

You know companies are so phony like you can sign your name on something and they'll beat you out of everything they can possibly get out of you . . . I think that's what happened to all the old groups too. Me personally, *What's Your Name* (Big Top 3079) was a very big record. But at the time there was so many loopholes in the music industry until you get your cut and they're living in big houses and buying Cadillacs off what you made . . . Sometimes money doesn't mean everything. Claps of hands can really lighten your heart . . . you just want to hear the hands of the people and it's nice that I'm in the show, 'cause I'm an oldie but goodie.[16]

The truth of Johnson's remarks is also applicable to the sad history of James Sheppard, leader of The Heartbeats and The Limelites. In 1962 Nom Music, a publishing subsidiary of Roulette Records, won a federal court case against him by proving that *Daddy's Home* was a copy of a 1956 hit *A Thousand Miles Away* (Rama 216, Hull 720) to which they owned the copyright. Sheppard had written and performed both songs. At a Madison Square concert in March 1970 The Drifters stopped in the middle of a medley of hits to dedicate *Please Stay* to 'the late James Sheppard who was a personal friend of all the Drifters here tonight and I'm sure to all of you out there.' His body had been found in his car on Belt Parkway on Long Island. He had been shot through the head.

In 1962 only Don and Juan, Ronnie and The Hi Lites and The Duprees were actively turning back the clock. The Earls, Vito and The Salutations and Sunny and The Sunliners survived until 1963 after which those who enjoyed singing in a similar fashion were forced to do so purely for their own amusement. They and their dwindling audience supported a small *a capella* industry in the North East. It was a phenomenon to which *Rolling Stone* devoted a large and interesting article in 1970.[17]

The swan-song of group harmony, however, temporarily disguised an increasingly important change that was taking place in popular music: the re-awakening of soul.

 POP SPOTLIGHT

THE DRIFTERS

I'LL TAKE YOU HOME

(Screen Gems-Columbia, BMI) (2:41)

I FEEL GOOD ALL OVER

(Roosevelt, BMI) (2:08)—Atlantic 2201

The Drifters are back with two winning items both in their usual soul style. Topper spotlights the lads on a teen-styled message song, on the order of their smash "Save the Last Dance for Me." It has a touch of folk-calypso, too. Side II is a catchy rhythm ditty with a strong lead handling the ballad with warmth. Two goodies.

 POP SPOTLIGHT

THE DRIFTERS

IF YOU DON'T COME BACK

(Trio-Cotillion, BMI) (2:10)

RAT RACE

(Trio-Cotillion, BMI) (2:10)—Atlantic 2191

The Drifters are back in with two solid follow-ups to "Broadway." They are in differing moods with a minor theme and arresting lyric idea on two. The second side is in the social conscience groove, but takes a quicker and wilder tempo.

From Billboard.

DRIFTING AWAY FROM YOU

Pundits have been attempting to define soul ever since 1959 when a record entitled *You're So Fine* (Unart 2013) crept into the national best-sellers. The group was called The Falcons, but they were not a 'bird' group in the accepted sense and the treatment they gave to such a trivial sentiment had not been heard before. It was a sad, wide open sound with pungent guitar-work and a full-bodied, slightly nasal lead singer named Joe Stubbs. The lyrics are simple: the object of the singer's attention is beautiful and belongs to him alone. Yet Stubbs's voice does not convey a feeling of triumphant possession; he sings as if he were heartbroken. The effect was both startling and immensely attractive. I tend to regard it as the first 'soul' record and, like most innovations in popular music, the first is usually the best. Joe Stubbs moved on to The Contours[1] whilst his brother Levi found success with The Four Tops. They and The Falcons came from Detroit, home of Tamla-Motown, which today typifies many of the least enjoyable characteristics of soul music.

Motown's emphasis on quality is indicated by one of their publicity pamphlets: 'In essence, each recording is "custom-made". A recording by any Motown artist must undergo stringent scrutiny for perfection of performance; perfection of production.' The sound of The Earls' bassman spluttering and choking on *Let's Waddle* (Old Town 1130) or, earlier still, The Gladiolas coming in as if they were drunk during the chorus of *Sweetheart Please Don't Go* (Excello 2101) would no longer escape the attention of those involved in the cutting of records. I mourned the passing of such quaint imperfections and also distrusted the ruthless efficiency which no longer created a personal expression from a combination of gospel and R&B. The element of spontaneity had made an enormous difference to the performance of those who had previously bastardised the blues or gospel. Producers at Motown still went into the studio with 'head' arrangements, but a battery of electronic aids transformed any vestige of raw simplicity into a slick, mechanical production. Soul now seemed to be a dishonest amalgam. Various performers began to use the same backing track for different songs and Tamla-Motown became synonymous with the word 'factory'. Paradoxically, the public consider technical perfection to be more important than bringing out the soul of the performer. Sixty per cent of Tamla-Motown's releases have been hits since the inauguration of the label and a glance at Appendix 2 illustrates their total domination of the R&B market during the late '60s.

Soul is not typified by the refinements of the recording studio alone. Instrumentation was also different: it was no longer used purely to accompany the singer. Melodic horn figures became as important as voices, and a thudding bass-line is now considered by Wexler to be *the* most important thing on hit soul records: 'That's what differentiates R&B from jazz. Also from pop music. When most of us go to record an R&B tune we look for a strong bass-line.'[2] The 'discotheque' sound of much recent soul music is characterised by the tight, well arranged mixture of heavy bass and staccato brass riffs. It is intended for dancing if not for listening. There lies the key to another crucial difference between today's soul and yesterday's R&B. Changing tastes in fashion and presentation have conspired to produce a new wave of groups. Zoot suits, top hat and tails or white gloves and phosphorescent bow-ties have been replaced by sharply creased hip huggers, cummerbunds or ruffled shirts. Soul groups are still required to look sharp but, above all else, they have to dance. The accent is no longer primarily aural but strictly visual. Black groups had always moved their hands in declamatory fashion. Those nearer comedy (Coasters, Royal Jokers, Cadillacs) had clowned about, whilst those singing pure harmony (Orioles, Lime-lites, Moonglows) frequently re-grouped around the microphone in mid-song. Throughout the '60s, however, each fresh group became proud of its very own corny dance routine. The decade was littered with their variations of the bump, the jerk, the twine, the fish, and so on. To keep in touch, groups from an earlier era, like The Vibrations, stood still whilst singing but felt compelled to close their performance with a masterful display of gymnastics. Watch The Temptations or The Four Tops; every limb is in perpetual motion, all is perfectly synchronised right down to the direction in which the last drop of sweat is propelled.

'What white man really understands all that silly choreography?' asked Robert Christgau.[3] Arnold Shaw provided a partial answer:

Doubtless, the current concern with choreography, not only among negro performers but a vast number of rock groups as well, is partly the consequence of today's advanced recording techniques . . . live performances can only approximate the effects achieved by overdubbing, mixing and the many sophisticated types of echo. To make up for the loss in aural impact singers are compelled to find ways of enhancing the visual thrust of their presentations.[4]

And so Berry Gordy had a school of choreography in which new signings to the Tamla-Motown complex were coached. While the live performance of soul depended upon the physical agility and, less often, the personal magnetism of those who sang it, the music continued to suffer. On record at least, soul could occasionally be more worthwhile. It could be happy, sad or mechanical – devoid of any emotion. It is especially good when it is sad, and superlative when the singer sounds sad though the situation demands that he be happy, which is why The Falcons' *You're So Fine* is a magnificent soul record. Other good ones include Wilson Pickett's *It's Too Late* (Double L 717), Garnet Mimms' *Cry Baby* (United Artists 629) and, most of all, Solomon Burke's slower numbers for Atlantic.

Bert Berns produced the Garnet Mimms record. In addition, he looked after Solomon Burke, made a searing revival of Burke's *Cry To Me* with Freddie Scott (Shout 211) and also produced The Jarmels' pioneering soul hit of 1961. They sang of *A Little Bit Of Soap* (Laurie 3098) 'used to wash away tears'. Apart from his initials, Berns had little in common with Burt Bacharach. A stocky man with a crop of tousled black hair, he was reminiscent of the paunchy, superannuated rock 'n' roller Gene Vincent; but Berns was a soul man. More remarkably, a white soul man. Before starting his own production company he had toiled as a record salesman, a music copyist and a session pianist. Impressed by his records with Mimms, The Isley Brothers and The Exciters, Atlantic signed Berns in 1963. If Bacharach smiled upon hearing his play-backs, Berns probably wept. Whereas the former had reduced The Drifters to saccharine puppets, in order to demonstrate his own genius, Berns brought an equally overbearing but noticeably different attitude to the music he produced. Despite a formal education at The Juillard School of Music, Berns managed to inject a convincing air of heartbreak and suffering into the majority of his records with black singers, including those of The Drifters.

Whilst Rudy Lewis had sung lead on some of The Drifters' biggest hits, the material was largely below par to the rhythm and blues enthusiast. There were odd exceptions like the underrated *What To Do* which illustrated what Lewis could do given a song by black writers – Treadwell and guitarist Billy Davis (whose real name is Abdul Samed). Incredibly, it had a harp solo, a really chunky beat and, most surprising of all, Lewis's low-register shrieks. His only solo recording, which, I feel, must have been produced by Berns, is a less enjoyable but valuable pointer to Lewis's hitherto submerged talent. *Baby, I Dig Love* (Atlantic 2193), recorded at the same session as *Rat Race*, had no strings but piano, organ and percussion only. It was ruined by a girl chorus whose tinny, computer-like chants spoil what could have been an interesting performance. The other side, written by Ertegun, was *I've Loved You So Long*, a slow, rambling, soul ballad without a shred of melody. I

Above: Baby, I Dig Love, *with* What to Do, *one of the best Drifters' sides with Rudy Lewis as lead.* Right: *a double-sided hit produced by Bert Berns.*

liked it, but neither side caused a stir. In summer, 1964, Lewis died.

The trade-marks of Berns' production work with The Drifters are first evident on *Didn't It* and *One Way Love*, but *Under The Boardwalk* is the nearest they came to recording the sort of soul classic mentioned earlier. Lewis' death, variously attributed to an overdose of drugs, choking himself during a meal or a heart-attack, had a profound effect upon the other members of the group. Their distress and Berns' talent for creating emotionally convincing records combined to turn *Under The Boardwalk* – basically a happy-go-lucky tune of summer love – into a memorable, moving song with overtones of loneliness and despair. Johnny Moore sings about fun but it is difficult to believe him. There is a mournful edge to his voice, a bitter, sad inflection which was never present on earlier records. Berns seemed to be instrumental in coaxing the truly soulful element out of numerous black singers. Before teaming up with Berns, Freddie Scott and Garnet Mimms had made a number of weak records and, when it came to soul, Moore's solo recordings were similarly insipid. His sides for Melic and Sue, often written for him by The Drifters' early guitarist Jimmy Oliver, should have been better than they were, but a regular girl chorus, a flute or a thin fairground organ resulted in unexceptional soul much akin to the work of Marv Johnson; not untuneful but uninspired, lightweight performances. *Under The Boardwalk* and its sequel, *Sand In My Shoes*, are Moore's best. Berns brought out a range that Moore had rarely shown before; he rises to a falsetto in a quite effortless manner. These records also had a 'bottom'. There were other voices behind Moore.

True, they were only chanting the title, but *Under The Boardwalk* was clearly a group recording. Since the time when the delicious bass voices of Ellsbury Hobbs and Tommy Evans had punctuated the otherwise smooth, sophisticated *Mexican Divorce* and *Please Stay* the feel of group participation had been largely absent from The Drifters' recordings. Two songs from the same session as *Under The Boardwalk* also illustrate the degree to which Berns was anxious to allow The Drifters to perform as a unit in which all had something to say. In *He's Just A Playboy* each sang a different note of the scale and Johnny Terry demonstrated that he possessed a masculine bass when allowed to use it. The flipside of *Under The Boardwalk* was recorded as a tribute to Rudy Lewis. Called *I Don't Want To Go On Without You*, it enabled the deep voice of Charles Thomas to be heard for the first time. He had occasionally sung lead baritone when the group were known as The Five Crowns, but since their change of name had been unable to compete with the succession of natural 'stars', Ben E King, Lewis and Johnny Moore who had all recorded as solo performers in addition to their role as lead singer with The Drifters.

Oddly, apart from a handful of meatier tunes including a revival of Solomon Burke's *You Can't Love Them All*, Thomas was rarely heard of subsequently. Had The Drifters concentrated upon soul with a capital 'S' as opposed to the diluted variety offered mainly by Motown and its imitators, Thomas would have been an obvious choice for the front position. But, according to Delehant, *Under The Boardwalk* finished The Drifters as a recording group. More accurately, they did not produce another record as good as *Boardwalk*, and although they continued to notch up five or six hits a year, these were increasingly unsuccessful in terms of sales.

Berns had taken over the dual role of producer-songwriter from Leiber and Stoller when they left Atlantic to concentrate upon the formation of their own Red Bird label. He too wished to branch out on his own, and, in conjunction with the Ertegun brothers and Jerry Wexler, he formed Bang Records in March 1965. In the beginning, they helped Berns by setting up promotion and distribution channels which allowed him sufficient time in which to continue to produce Atlantic's acts, including Barbara Lewis, Esther Phillips and The Drifters. During this period, The Drifters' records benefited from the arrangements of black orchestra leaders including Teacho Wilshire (*Saturday Night At The Movies*, *At The Club*) and pianist-arranger Bert Keyes, who directed the orchestra on *Chains Of Love* and *Come On Over To My Place*. Also apparent, though not in an earthy, uninhibited fashion, was Berns' interest in Spanish music. He went out of his way to sign Spanish-speaking performers for Bang and thought that the market should be recognised as an important sales source. His affection for such rhythms was reflected throughout his career. On the back of his best known composition, The Isley Brothers' *Twist And Shout* (Wand 124), was an instrumental workout of the same tune. Berns called it *Spanish Twist*. His only other world-wide hit was *My Girl Sloopy* or *Hang On Sloopy*. It too relied on a choppy, instantly catchy beat for its success with both the black audience (The Vibrations, Atlantic 2221) and an international but primarily white audience (The McCoys, Bang 506). In a way, Berns simply updated the Cuban Guajira beat which Leiber and Stoller had introduced to their work with The Drifters. From *Vaya Con Dios* in 1963 to *Spanish Lace* in 1964 to *You Can't Love Them All* in 1966, The Drifters' records possessed an undertow of insidious Latin American rhythms in both slow and up-tempo numbers.

The Bang label was primarily for white pop artists or ethnic Spanish performers but Berns wanted to diversify. Atlantic allowed him to take over complete control of the label, and immediately he set up an R&B subsidiary called Shout on which he placed greater emphasis. He signed a host of good, lesser known soul performers and picked up R&B masters from local labels throughout the East. Shout was exclusively for black artists and by concentrating on their production Berns was no longer able to give his full attention to Atlantic's acts. Before redeeming himself with a number of near-brilliant heavy soul records by, amongst others, George Freeman, Freddie Scott and Bobby Harris for Shout, Berns suffered a momentary lapse of taste. Perhaps at the dictate of higher authority, who wanted to see The Drifters performing on the supper club circuit, Berns produced an album entitled 'The Good Life With The Drifters'. The group had been an inevitable choice for early rock 'n' roll package tours but these had dwindled at the same time as rock 'n' roll itself began to change. The payola inquiry at various Governmental levels also contributed to its waning popularity. Groups like The Drifters were forced to perform in small ghetto clubs – the 'chittlin' circuit' – which normally permitted struggling or forgotten

R&B singers to eke out a living. By 1963, the package tour was making a comeback, but to a group like The Drifters it meant sharing a bill and a gross of as much as $500,000 with fifteen other acts. In the space of three days, they had to be at The Municipal Auditorium, Norfolk, The Keil Opera House, St Louis, or The Civic Center in Baltimore. To any performer it could be a gruelling existence. The Coasters had found that, by recording an album of standards under the title of 'One by One' (Atco 33-123), the road to the more remunerative cabaret dates was brought a little nearer. But for The Drifters 'The Good Life' failed. Some of the songs on it – *Desafinado*, *Quando Quando Quando* – reflected Berns' continuing taste for Spanish influences but, like the remainder of the album's contents, they were unadventurously performed standards. The orchestrations were as lifeless and as boring as the songs themselves and the album did nothing to capture the wealthy patrons of the Las Vegas clubs at whom it was presumably aimed. The Drifters also suffered from a lack of exposure on national television networks, particularly adult shows. The most they could achieve was an occasional appearance on a teen-orientated television show like 'Shindig'. Unlike The Supremes or The Temptations, The Drifters were not destined for super-stardom. Their constantly changing personnel may have worked against them in this respect. The audience found it difficult to adore a group whose faces changed every time they were seen. The Drifters never made The Copacabana but, on 22 March 1965, they arrived in Britain for a ballroom tour.

British audiences acknowledged the fact that, by 1965, the group had sold fifteen million records. They were treated in the manner that befits star performers and The Drifters were happy to oblige. They stayed at the Cumberland Hotel and mimed *At The Club* on 'Thank Your Lucky Stars', the current popular music television programme. Thomas regaled the press with how he had been to 'Buck House' to shoot snaps of the Queen while Billy Davis regularly repeated a story about how he had scraped the manufacturer's name from his guitar because they had refused to pay for the advertising he gave them. They played the Pigalle, the Strand Lyceum and the Starlite Room, Wembley. A succession of fancy dance routines accompanied each methodical performance. They sang seven of their machine-tooled, market-tested hits and the audience wanted to hear them; as far as they were concerned, the group's predictability was a talent to be applauded. Oddly, a number of rock 'n' roll and blues artists also toured this country during the same month. The wild, raw and totally uninhibited exhibitionism of Screaming Jay Hawkins, Buddy Guy, Larry Williams and Johnny 'Guitar' Watson provided an effective contrast to the polished but mechanical Drifters. Moreover, in January 1966, The Original Drifters toured Britain and, for many, effectively usurped affections for, if not memories of, the group on Atlantic.

Top left: *Screamin' Jay Hawkins – Rock 'n' Roll Clown*. Bottom left: *The Original Drifters, Gerhart Thrasher, Bobby Hendricks, Bobby Lee Hollis, Bill Pinkney*. Above: *The Original Drifters, Bobby Lee Hollis, Gerhart Thrasher, Andrew Thrasher, Bill Pinkney*.

The Original Drifters were largely the same group which had acted as pall-bearers to the coffin in which Screamin' Jay Hawkins had been carried on stage during the halcyon days of rock 'n' roll. When dismissed by Treadwell in 1958, Hendricks, Thrasher, Hughes and Pinkney continued to perform under the auspices of The Universal Attractions Booking Agency. Gerhart Thrasher's brother, Andrew, took Hughes' place but later retired to look after a small grocery shop, whilst Hendricks left in search of a solo career.[5] David Baughn and Bobby Lee

The Original Drifters in action, 1966. Gerhart Thrasher, Bobby Hendricks, Bobby Lee Hollis, Bill Pinkney.

Hollis[6] replaced them. Again, Baughn was unfortunate. He left without making any new records and is now believed to be on skid row.[7] In fact, six years elapsed before The Original Drifters were able to interest another recording company. Pinkney had not seen the inside of a recording studio since 1958 when, with a group he called The Turks, he cut two sides for Sam Phillips in Memphis. The record *After The Hop/Sally Got A Sister* (Phillips International 3524) was a belated sequel to Danny and The Juniors' *At The Hop*. It was written by Pinkney and instrumentalist, Bill Justis and it failed completely. In 1964, Pinkney and his Original Drifters cut *I Do The Jerk/Don't Call Me* (Fontana S1956) with Hollis and, in place of Baughn, Jimmy Lewis taking the lead vocals. Despite a production by James Brown it was a routine, undistinguished soul performance with little to commend it. Two years later, a second disc, *I Found Some Lovin'/The Masquerade Is Over* (Veep 1264), made an equally negligible impact. Between each release, The Original Drifters toured Britain with Bobby Hendricks who had returned to take the lead position from Jimmy Lewis.[8]

Their performances brought tears to the eyes of some but bewilderment to the majority. Compelled, by public expectation, to sing the songs of their hit-producing namesakes, they brought a fervent mixture of rough gospel influences and polished 'bird'-group harmony to such incongruous material as *Up On The Roof* or *Memories Are Made Of This*. Better yet was their own *Ruby Baby* or revivals of songs from a similarly early period, particularly *I Love You For Sentimental Reasons*, *Shout*, *The Night Time Is The Right Time* or *Only You*. Thrasher, thrice-married, world weary, all his life on the road, was, nevertheless, far from spent. 'Drinking his food' had taken its toll but he still sang loud and strong. Hendricks just stood still, opened his mouth and let fly with his incredible octave-juggling tenor voice. An early James Brown number was the nearest concession to current soul music, and here again they had got their priorities right. 'Have you tried Clyde McPhatter?' screamed Pinkney. 'Have you tried Jackie Wilson? Have you tried James Brown? Now *Try Me*!'

Steve Richards wrote of a performance at a Manchester all-nighter:

By the end, the audience were clapping, shouting and stamping for more. More came – via *Stand By Me* and *Sentimental Reasons* . . . the crowds' enthusiasm made it impossible for the group to return again but two of them – Thrasher and Hollis – rocked on for another five minutes of *Stand By Me*. This was quality rock 'n' roll.[9]

In preference to the local YMCA the group stayed at the above writer's flat where, at their request, the record-player featured nothing but 'bird' groups and their hits with Clyde McPhatter. Pinkney was observed to persistently replace the stylus at the beginning of The Orioles *It's Too Soon To Know*. The Original Drifters made a second tour of Britain and Bobby Hendricks also toured as solo performer but, on arrival in June 1967, Pinkney brought unwelcome news. He thought Thrasher had permanently retired, whilst Hendricks had gone solo once again. In their place was a new group[10] with Pinkney singing lead baritone: 'After fifteen years with various groups you get to be able to sing anything – like taking candy from a baby.' On 25 July 1970 *Billboard* reported that Bill Pinkney and The Soul Exciters were appearing at The Seven Seas Lounge, Miami. With the exception of McPhatter, it was the last to be heard of any of The Original Drifters. Moreover, things were not going at all well for Treadwell's Drifters in New York.

Berns' last production was *Aretha* issued on the flip of the spirited, if Motownish *Baby, What I Mean*. He died of a heart-attack at his hotel residence on 31 December 1967 and, not long afterwards, Teacho Wilshire also passed away. Deprived of their major soul producer and chief arranger-director, it seemed as if Atlantic scarcely knew what to do with The Drifters. Each forthcoming release was the result of an

independent production deal. Ronnie Savoy of Suron Productions had made a number of vocal records with MGM (for whom he made two sizeable hits in 1959 and 1960) and Atlantic. Since then he had produced lesser known soulsters including The Fantastic Four (Ric-Tic), Brenda Jo Harris (Revilot) and Jesse Henderson (Gold Dust). But he had yet to find real success as a producer and The Drifters *Ain't It The Truth/Up Jumped The Devil*, which he also wrote, did not help him. *Still Burning In My Heart* was another, by now familiar, Motown imitation with a complex arrangement and fuzz-box guitar. 'Music to go mad by' said one reviewer. One of the producers, Lou Courtney, had lived on dance crazes whilst the other, Bob Bateman, had come down in the world since producing Wilson Pickett's *It's Too Late*.

Of course, the line-up was changing all the time. Eugene Pearson

Left: *not The Original Drifters, but soul-group The Invitations, who masqueraded as The Drifters*. Above: *the author investigates*.

and Johnny Terry had been replaced by Rick Sheppard and William Brent. Brent left and in came Dan Dandridge. Dandridge left; in came Bill Fredericks. Sheppard was drafted; in came Butch Leake. Charles Thomas left and, according to one source,[11] the new bass singer could have been Don Thomas. However, Ritchie Yorke, reviewing a performance at Toronto's Friars Tavern in December 1968, stated: 'Between sets, Moore said the group had been on a month's tour with Aretha Franklin. He introduced Milton Turner, who had replaced Charles Thomas.'[12] Perhaps there was a personnel for live performances and another for studio recordings. In any event it became impossible to keep track of such furious personnel changes. Not that it mattered a great deal; they all sang soul, sometimes with an awareness of the new, self-conscious Afro-America. Bert Berns may have been one of the first to recognise the struggle for black identity when he wrote and produced *Up In The Streets Of Harlem* for The Drifters in 1966. Four years later, black aspirations had established a voice in the lyrics and performance of R&B songs. The Temptations consult a Swahili glossary for their latest records; The Drifters wear natural, unstraightened hair and sing of *Black Silk*. But, to use a turned phrase from *R&B Magazine* 'black was beautiful' when The Moonglows sang; when the left-over Drifters sing, it is merely uninteresting.

1966 and 1967 were the greatest years in Atlantic's history with sales

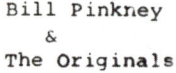

Left: *Bill Pinkney and The Originals: Pinkney, Albert Fortson, Wallace Ezzard, Benny Anderson, with guitarist Mark Williams.* Right: *The Drifters, 1967: Charles Thomas, Bill Fredericks, Rick Sheppard, Johnny Moore.*

up 50% over previous years, yet The Drifters' contribution was virtually nil. Jerry Wexler was commuting from Miami to Muscle Shoals, preoccupied with the production and promotion of the label's solo soul giants – Wilson Pickett and Aretha Franklin. The only groups to get a look in were white: The Young Rascals and the so-called progressive, heavy rock groups: Led Zeppelin, Iron Butterfly and The Cream. From The Drifters, only four singles in three years. What had gone wrong?

On 17 January 1948, *Billboard* carried the following paragraph:

New York, Jan 10 – New diskery, Atlantic Records, formed prior to the Petrillo ban, will debut next week. Initial platters will include wax by bassist Eddie Safranski, warbler Melrose Colbert, Bob Howard and The Tiny Grimes Quintet. The waxery was organised by Herb Abramson, former artist and rep director for National records, Ahmet Ertegun and Dr Vahdi Sabit. The firm which claims to have accrued some 200 pre-deadline masters of the race and hot jazz variety, is now busy setting up national distribution.

Atlantic had arrived at a time when independent, non-establishment record companies were burgeoning. Simultaneously, the late '40s also saw a proliferation of black radio stations. The war had brought massive shifts of population; blacks had increased their spending power by working at defence armaments plants and the formation of BMI (in 1940) enabled new writers, in particular, black writers, to reap royalties where they had previously been barred from doing so by the established publishing houses. These, and other factors too complex to enlarge upon here, enabled the independent labels to dominate the popular market rapidly. Atlantic was one of the first; they were largely responsible for the development of popular R&B from country blues and, prior to 1953, had had hits in the black market with Frank 'Floorshow' Culley, The Cardinals, Ruth Brown, The Clovers and Sticks McGhee. Louisiana convict, Leadbelly, with his posthumous success *Goodnight Irene* (917) and one-time Kansas City bartender, Joe Turner's million-selling *Chains Of Love* (939) were particularly significant.

Other emergent independent R&B labels included Savoy (Newark), Chess (Chicago), King (Cincinnatti) and, in California, which during World War II underwent a great black migration, Imperial, Specialty, Exclusive, Modern and Aladdin. Of those who remain active, Atlantic is the most popular today. When referring to the Beatles, Phyl Garland wrote . . . 'they re-introduced to this country [America] a modified version of Presley's sound, noticeably altered by the use of group singing (through The Clovers, Spaniels, Coasters, Drifters and others) . . .' It is significant that, of the four groups Miss Garland mentions, three were on the Atlantic label or its subsidiary, Atco. As one of the largest independents, Atlantic had fewer distribution problems than those which hindered Dootone, Onyx, Whirlin' Disc and many smaller labels which concentrated upon group products. Numerous good groups, including The Five Satins, failed to create an indelible impression because they jumped from label to label, skipping about amongst a hotch-potch of minor independents who could afford payola in a make or break gamble but could not command the widespread distribution which Atlantic enjoyed. In part, The Drifters impressive roster of double-sided hits is due to Atlantic's promotional ability and the respect they had built up 'in the field'. If *Rat Race* did not seem to be selling as well as it should, Atlantic promptly alerted distributors and disc-jockeys to the possibilities of the other side. They soon became the number one R&B label in the USA.

Between 1950 and 1966, Atlantic had well over 100 Top Ten R&B hits, far surpassing the 64 successes achieved by Mercury, their closest rival. It was a superiority to which The Drifters had contributed more than any of their other artists. By 1966 the group – with or without McPhatter – had achieved a total of 23 records in the R&B Top Ten best-sellers. (Lagging far behind were The Clovers (16), The Midnighters (13), The Platters (10) and, joint equal with The Dominoes, The Supremes (9).) But, in 1966, the hits stopped coming. Their sporadic

The Drifters' arranger-director Teacho Wilshire, top left, *and producers*: top right: *Phil Spector;* bottom left: *Jerry Wexler and Bert Berns;* bottom right: *Lou Courtney;* opposite: *Bob Bateman and Ronnie Savoy. Russell Byrd (pseudonym of Bert Berns) recording on his own.*

RUSSELL BYRD
★★★★ Little Bug—WAND 121—A lonely fellow with no one to talk to finds himself talking to a little bug here, as he explains his lonely life. Attractive tune and moving performance make this a record with a chance. Watch. (Mellin, BMI) (3:14)

★★★ Nights of Mexico—(Mellin, BMI) (2:53)

---

releases were given little or no promotion; I do not recollect an advertisement in any of the trade papers, except one for *Still Burning In My Heart* – and, unless one knew better, one could be forgiven for assuming that Atlantic were hanging fire, merely waiting for The Drifters contract to expire before writing them off as a once worth-while but no longer indispensable acquisition.

It was an unusual situation for a company which had always pushed the product it believed in. After he left Atlantic, Ben E King gave a valuable and candid insight into the bitter-sweet nature of the disaffection that can arise from working with the same people for over a decade.

I didn't really want to leave Atlantic. But I find companies are like a husband and wife. Eventually you get to a point where there's really very little you can do for each other. Although you're married and you love each other dearly, but then there's still something else, and you have to, like, sacrifice. And one has to leave. So I had to. I didn't so much want to but I found that if I would have stayed there, I would have accepted things out of friendship, and I didn't want that. I didn't want a recording session because they felt, well, this is Benny and he's been here eleven years and we'll give him one.

They're very beautiful, very honest, very true people. You couldn't find better people to be with. They've stayed with an artist when he's been going down, down, and they've stayed with him. I said to myself, I'll give myself one more record . . . and if that don't happen, well to keep them from investing in me, and to keep me from feeling that I'm sinking, I'll have to leave.[13]

In comparison with King, Johnny Moore (who is still on Atlantic with The Drifters) seemed less than honest. 'We don't really need it [another hit]' said Moore, 'When you've been in the business fifteen years people accept you.'[14] Do people 'accept' The Midnighters? Do they 'accept' Lee Andrews and The Hearts, The Cadillacs? Who are The Cadillacs? Occasionally, a specialist musical magazine will turn out a splendid appreciation ten years too late. More often, but scarcely frequently, groups like these will appear at a local fairground 'Blast From The Past

Revue' or an annual 'Golden Oldies Show' at The Apollo Theater in Harlem. Here they will gladden the hearts of a comparatively small band of devotees – the archaeologists of rock 'n' roll. Otherwise, the day arrives when it is all over. The Drifters no longer sell records. Their audience has been induced to like someone else and, as the editor of *Downbeat* once remarked, there is nothing in this world as useless as a rock 'n' roll star who no longer sells. Johnny Moore may soon be dreaming of a comeback and, while he remains with Atlantic, he may be lucky. Lee Andrews has no recording contract. He also dreams of a comeback but without any hope of one.

The Drifters will be remembered with affection as long as people possess their records, but if they are to be successful in the future, they will have to find a lead singer with the talent and personality of Clyde McPhatter, as well as producers and writers comparable in stature to those I have discussed. The Ertegun brothers, Leiber and Stoller, Wexler and Berns were all giants in the recording industry. Their fresh and original ideas enabled The Drifters to stay ahead of popular trends and the success of the group was largely due to the fact that their producers and writers were motivated more by musical considerations than anything else. Leiber was not impressed with promotors, distributors or disc-jockeys; 'I'm not a businessman', he has said, 'I'm a songwriter.' Of Wexler, who replaced Abramson soon after Atlantic's inception, he stated: 'He loved music, he loved jazz, he loved the blues.'[15] Wexler and Ahmet Ertegun produced The Drifters from 1953 to 1956, after which they were usually on hand to offer friendly advice to whoever succeeded them. Said Leiber '(they) would sometimes drop in on a session and sit in the booth and dig the session. And usually love it. Sometimes Jerry would say "Man I think you need a little more bass" or "I think that drum is a little bit too crisp".' But The Drifters' early records show no indication of such considerate interference. Bearing in mind his eulogy to Phil Spector and his opinion of Leiber and Stoller – 'why don't they write their names with letters of fire in the sky' – Wexler's own lack of flamboyance is implicit in his own words in *Fusion*:

And there's the other kind of producer, the other style, who beats the bushes to find a Sam Cooke, you know, or a Coasters, or whatever, who then helps bring this thing together, get the artist into the studio, get the right sound, and guide his career. Personally, that's always been the thrust of Atlantic Records. We've been interested, you know, this may seem a little simplistic, it may seem almost too passé: we've been interested in one thing at Atlantic . . . Singers. I mean, bel canto has been our byword . . . And another thing: we've been the specialists in the single artist, in an era when groups were in. In those years, we didn't have too many groups. We had a few, The Coasters, The Drifters. But the ones we had lasted, you know, it seems damn near forever.

Ertegun and Wexler did not produce so much as supervise. Mickey 'Guitar' Baker, Stone or Henry Van Walls on piano and, perhaps, Connie Kay on drums cooked up a scintillating rhythm and the singers generally sang how and when they pleased. McPhatter took all sorts of liberties with the lyrics and melody in a way that was denied to Rudy Lewis under Bacharach. Ertegun and Wexler stayed in the background and allowed The Drifters to perform in whatever manner was most natural to them. They enjoyed the authenticity of what they heard, and although what they enjoyed also had a financially profitable side effect they were blues fans and record collectors first; businessmen second. Don Heckman wrote:

Their [the Ertegun brothers] understanding of the place of race music and the blues in the total perspective of American music came to them intuitively. The sons of a one-time Turkish ambassador to the United States helped to perform a valuable cultural service. As did Baudelaire with Edgar Allen Poe and Hughes Panassié with jazz, they brought Americans face to face with another of their own art forms.[16]

Historically, the combination of McPhatter and Ertegun/Wexler will not be matched. After 1960, the strength of The Drifters' material has contributed to the general impression that, as a group, they have been particularly influential. But, apart from the widespread impact of *There Goes My Baby*, only little-known pop – soul acts – Dobie Gray, The O'Jays, Richard Mandel – have actually set out to achieve a similar 'Drifters' sound.

Whatever their respective merits, lyricists as far apart as Jerry Leiber and Hal David, or tunesmiths as stylistically distinct from one another as Mike Stoller and Burt Bacharach enabled The Drifters to start trends, adapt to new styles, or survive the changing styles of not only R&B groups but popular music as a whole. But whether it was a jubilant twelve-bar blues or a mature ballad reflecting serious aspects of life, the group's material was always being covered by other – usually white – performers in search of easy royalties. The American covers of The Drifters' early hits by Johnny Ray or Dorothy Collins were only marginally more distasteful than those inflicted upon British ears by a plethora of home-grown teen idols who warrant no more than a footnote.[17] Jimmy Justice virtually impersonated Ben E King, but the remainder merely copied the ideas of the original arranger or producer. All effectively destroyed any chance of The Drifters duplicating their American chart record in Britain.

Influence – as distinct from an attraction to record The Drifters' songs – is best judged by a comment from McPhatter, who started it all eighteen years ago:

There were guys like Jackie Wilson – who replaced me in The Dominoes

– Ben E King, Bobby Hendricks, Dee Clark and Donnie Elbert, Smokey Robinson of The Miracles and just about every lead singer of vocal groups in America that have come to me and said they have patterned themselves after me.

Amongst those who have enjoyed Top Ten R&B hits, McPhatter could have included Sammy Turner, Eugene Church, Wade Flemons, Jimmy Charles and Marv Johnson. Rock 'n' roll enthusiasts – as defined by the British classification – should also pay homage. Jerry Lee Lewis, Elvis Presley, Little Richard and Ronnie Hawkins have all recorded songs McPhatter wrote or originally recorded. In 1962, the world was shaken by *The Twist*; Hank Ballard had simply put inferior words to the tune of *Whatcha Gonna Do*. But Ballard was being copied by Chubby Checker, and few saw the irony of the situation. Most important, McPhatter took hold of The Inkspots' simple major chord harmonies, drenched them in call-and-response patterns and sang as if he were back in church. In doing so he created a revolutionary musical style from which – thankfully – popular music will never recover.

In 1968, McPhatter sold his house and came to Britain. In that year, royalties from Atlantic and Progressive Music amounted to just over £1000, but his live performance was deemed to be worth sometimes £80, more often £15. He made some disconcertingly nervous personal appearances, cut a few sides for British record companies and went back home after a charge of 'loitering with intent' was happily dismissed. Nevertheless, it was an ignominious period in a career which had contributed so much to popular music. Hopefully, it is not the end. At the time of writing a new album on Decca ('Welcome Home' – DL 75231) has met with good reviews and, although the arrangements leave much to be desired, his voice is as exciting as ever.

The rock 'n' roll heritage is in danger of being overlooked. From the late '40s, when it began to emerge from a complex stock of 'bird' groups, blues, gospel and country music, it has been surrounded by a world of colourful, supremely talented performers. Many of these are already long-forgotten. I do not believe this fate will overtake Clyde McPhatter and The Drifters.

Further Reading

If readers require more factual information it is readily available in a number of magazines which I unreservedly recommend. Those concerned primarily with RHYTHM AND BLUES, particularly earlier group styles, include: *Record Exchanger*, Box 2144, Anaheim, California 92804; *R&B Magazine*, Box 1229, Santa Monica, California 90406; *Shout*, 46 Slades Drive, Chislehurst, Kent; *Stormy Weather*, 95 Moss Avenue, No 5, Oakland, California 94611.

SOUL MUSIC, including useful if less specialist coverage of current black groups, is to be found in: *Afro-Star* (formerly *R 'n' B World*) 35 West 56th Street, New York 10019; *Blues and Soul*, 12 New Burlington Street, London W1; *Soul*, 8271 Melrose Avenue, Los Angeles, California 90046; *Soul Sounds*, 1133 Broadway, New York 10010.

Notes

The Church is on Fire

1 Bill Johnson, 'Deep are the Roots', *The World of Soul*, Billboard Publication, 1968, p. 32.
2 Don Light, 'Gospel enters the Mainstream', *The World of Gospel Music*, Billboard Publication, 1967, p. 8.
3 Light is president of a talent agency whose performers include ex-Governor of Louisiana Jimmie Davis, The Chuck Wagon Gang and The Oakridge Boys.
4 *Oh Happy Day* was originally issued on Century 31016 in April 1969 and later picked up by Buddah, who distributed the record on yet another label, Pavilion 2001. The record made Number 1 on both national and R&B charts in June 1969. Edwin R Hawkins played piano and arranged and conducted the choir.
5 Phyl Garland, *The Sound of Soul*, Henry Regnery Co., Chicago, 1969, p. 25.
6 *The World of Religious Music*, Billboard Publication, 1965, p. 82.
7 Vic Fredericks [ed.], *Who's Who in Rock 'n' Roll*, Frederick Fell, Inc., New York, 1958, p. 26.
8 Charles Keil, *Urban Blues*, University of Chicago Press, 1966, p. 158.
9 James Weldon Johnson, *The Autobiography of an Ex-Colored Man*, Knopf, New York, 1912.
10 Robinson is full-time pastor at The Macedonia Baptist Church, East St Louis. His sermons (Jewel LPs 0001 and 0004) culminate in massed congregational singing.

Ornithology

1 Joe Van Loan (first tenor), Tommy Evans (bass), Louis Heywood (second tenor), Louis Frazier (baritone), Ricky Cannon (baritone), Joe Medlin (baritone), 'Boots' Bowers (bass), Jimmy Stewart and Paul Van Loan. The line-up preferred by most collectors is that of Ricks, Suttles, Puzey and Maithe Marshall (who replaced Ollie Jones).
2 Jessie Walker, *The Apollo Theater Story*, Apollo Operations, Inc., New York, 1966, p. 4B.
3 Which accounts for the rarity of such recordings today and the high prices they command in auctions. Old group records, including several by The Orioles, have been known to fetch sums from $40 to $250.
4 *The World of Soul*, Billboard Publication, 1967, p. 48.
5 *Tweedlee Dee* (Atlantic 1047), an R&B hit for Lavern Baker, was copied note for note by Georgia Gibbs, who reaped enormous sales with her version in the white market. Similarly Dorothy Collins' version of Clyde McPhatter's *Seven Days* (Atlantic 1981) gained national acclaim at the expense of the original.
6 Fredericks, p. 91.
7 Freed's defence of black music had incurred the wrath of the establishment. Whilst charges of inciting to riot and anarchy were dismissed in 1958, he was subsequently victimised for his part in the 'payola' scandals. In September 1962 he was charged with having taken bribes from six record companies. He pleaded guilty to part of the charge and received a six month suspended sentence and a $300 fine. He moved to the West Coast in an unsuccessful attempt to revive his career but died of uremia in a Palm Springs hospital on 20 January 1965. He had done more than anyone to spread the gospel of rock 'n' roll and few recognised his contribution to the advancement of black performers. But the *New York Post* editorialised: 'He died depending on whether you get an up tempo version or a slow blues, of either a broken heart or too much whiskey.'
8 Unpublished interview with Lynn McCutcheon.
9 The Dominoes continued to record for King, Jubilee, Decca, Liberty and Melbourne. Eugene Mumford, who had been lead singer with The Larks, replaced Jackie Wilson.
10 *Blues and Soul Monthly Music Review* 22, September 1969.
11 Charlie Gillett, *The Sound of The City*, Outerbridge and Dienstfrey, New York, 1969, pp. 178-9.

Rockin 'n' Driftin'

1 Fortunately, Til did not acquiesce. After singles for Vee-Jay and Roulette in 1956 and 1957 he re-cut some of his old songs for Charlie Parker Records with a new group of Orioles – Gerald Gregory, Billy Taylor, Delton McCall and Mundell Lowe (g). Their album – 'The Modern Sounds of The Orioles' (PLP 816) – was, in fact, a close recreation of Til's earlier sound. In 1964 he re-recorded more oldies for Sutton in New York leading to the release of a fresh *Crying in the Chapel* (Lana 109). Til now records for RCA Victor under the supervision of Robert Stroud.
2 Jim Delehant, 'The Rise and Fall of the Vocal Groups', *Crawdaddy*, January 1967.
3 The four songs which were not cover records were: (2) *Crazy Otto Medley*, Johnny Maddox (Dot); (4) *Melody of Love*, Billy Vaughn (Dot); (6) *Ballad of Davy Crockett*, Bill Hayes (Cadence); (9) *Melody of Love*, David Carroll (Mercury).
4 *Record Exchanger* 1:3, June 1970.
5 Monotones interviewed by Lenny Goldberg, *Stormy Weather* 1, July 1970.
6 Gene Lees, 'The Teenage Idol Blues', unknown source.
7 The Hill Toppers covered *Only You* for Dot but their 'cover' version was not as successful as the original.
8 Sonny Woods interviewed by Lynn McCutcheon, *Record Exchanger* 1:4, August/September 1970.
9 A not uncommon event. When Tony Williams left The Platters, Mercury auditioned sixty vocalists before choosing Sonny Turner, whose voice was almost identical.
10 Baughn's penetrating voice was heard on many of The Checkers' records for King including, in all probability, the penultimate verse of *The White Cliffs of Dover* (King 4675), one of the all-time great old group sounds with a bass lead, and a regional R&B success in January 1954. In the same year he formed his own group, The Harps. The two titles they made for Savoy, *I Won't Cry* and *You'll Pay* (Savoy 1178), have appeared in label listings as 'Little David and

his Harp', which may well have misled group admirers into thinking that the credits hid the identity of a country bluesman. Baughn gave a creditable imitation of Clyde McPhatter on both self-penned sides.
11 Oliver, from Buffalo, was rarely able to reveal his instrumental dexterity with The Drifters. Until 1958 the group's records were essentially tributes to the human voice and their powerful and vivid harmonies rendered guitar solos superfluous. Nonetheless, Oliver had recorded prolifically since 1948, when his work was showcased on *Stealin' Home* (Rainbow 10063). Remaining in New York, he made more sides including *Slim Jim* (Port 70016) in 1957 and *The Sneak* (Sue 707) in 1958. Years later, Sue released an album (LP1041) featuring Oliver's workouts on a selection of Tamla-Motown songs. He also wrote a number of Clyde McPhatter's Mercury sides and both men formed a publishing venture, Olimac. As recently as 1970 Oliver enjoyed success as a producer, being responsible for the small hit *The Cat Walk* by The Village Soul Choir (Abbott 2010).
12 It has been mooted (in *Blues and Soul*) that Moore sang with The Hornets on records for Savoy in 1949. No such records exist, and the lead vocal on discs by The Hornets on Flash and States (in 1954) is not by Moore.
13 Jerry Wexler interviewed by Bobby Abrams and Sandy Pearlman, *Fusion* 36, June 1970.

'Beat Concerto' *v.* 'Oldies but Goodies'

1 Jerry Leiber interviewed by Michael March, *Fusion* 39, 21 August 1970.
2 Black groups, like The Orioles in 1950 and The Moonglows in 1956, had recorded with strings before, but such occasions were both comparatively rare and commercially unsuccessful.
3 Arthur Jacobs, *A New Dictionary of Music*, Penguin, London, 1958, p. 379.
4 Bob Plotnick, 'Platter Chatter', *Big Beat* 12, June 1966, p. 9.
5 Roy Stanton, *Shout* 55, May 1970, p. 5.
6 *Billboard*, 12 July 1969.
7 A deliberate over-simplification in the interests of brevity.
8 *Billboard*, 25 July 1970.
9 Records by Johnny Williams on Kent and Cub are probably by the same artist. Others by John Williams (Sansu) are not.
10 Nik Cohn, *Wop Bop A Loo Bop A Lop Bam Boom*, Paladin, London, 1970, pp. 38–9.
11 Herbie Cox interviewed by Lenny Goldberg, *Stormy Weather* 1, June 1970.
12 Charlie Gillett, *Soul Music* 7, 3 March 1968.
13 Bob Rolontz, *Record World*, 13 February 1965.
14 Maurice Williams' *Stay* was a hit in November 1960. His group, The Zodiacs, had the original version of the hit record *Little Darlin'* under the name of The Gladiolas (Excello 2101).
15 Tony Armato interviewed by Lenny Goldberg, *Stormy Weather* 1, June 1970.
16 Claude Johnson interviewed by Lenny Goldberg, *Stormy Weather* 1, June 1970.
17 Lenny Kaye and Ed Ward, 'Acappella', *Rolling Stone* 56, 16 April 1970, pp. 40–1.

Drifting Away From You

1 In 1970 Joe Stubbs returned to best-selling status with 100 Proof Aged In Soul, a group on Hot Wax, one of the Holland–Dozier–Holland labels.
2 Claude Hall, 'Atlantic Helped Pave the Way,' *The World of Soul*, Billboard Publication, June 1967, p. 16.
3 Robert Christgau, 'Two Nights in the Life of a Soul Man', *Cheetah Magazine*, New York, 1968.
4 Arnold Shaw, 'Choreography and Soul,' *The World of Soul*, Billboard Publication, August 1968, pp. 42–3.
5 In 1958 Bobby Hendricks launched the independent New York Sue label with his recording of the Jimmy Oliver composition *Itchy Twitchy Feeling* (Sue 706), a traditional rock 'n' roll sound with a frantic vocal and tearaway sax solo. Rock 'n' roll leanings were also evident in his other Sue singles – eight in all – including *Molly B Goode* (708), a Chuck Berry take-off. *Sincerely Your Lover*, the reverse of his only other hit for Sue – *Little John Green* (717) – was a heart-felt soul ballad with a spoken introduction by the guitarist, Oliver. In 1961 Hendricks moved to Mercury, where the producer seems to have been impressed by the success of Clarence Henry. Hendrick's fragile tenor fails to come to terms with the jazzy big band which Mercury supplied for the Charlie Rich tune *I'm Comin' Home* (71881), the more successful of his two records for them. Other titles, like those cut for MGM in 1963, remain unissued and Hendricks joined The Original Drifters. In a so far unsuccessful attempt to re-establish a solo career, he made *Go On Home Girl* (Williams 1) for Aubrey Williams in June 1969.
6 Bobby Lee Hollis, who was born in Carolina in 1939, had sung gospel material with several childhood groups before joining The Sunbeams in 1954. The group (Hollis, Billy Davis, Johnny and Bobby Coleman) made *Come Back Baby/Tell Me Why* (Herald 451) but broke up shortly after the record's release. After three unissued titles for King, including Chuck Willis's *It's Too Late*, Hollis cut one solo recording for Juggy Murray in New York. To avoid confusion with Bobby Lee (ex-lead of The Fiestas), the two sides – *Wonderful Baby* and *Shook* (Sue 721) – were issued under the pseudonym of Johnny Pancake. 'Murray liked looking into recipe books', said Hollis, whose single did not sell well. He now lives in Miami and is no longer active in music.
7 According to Peter Burns, *Blues and Soul Monthly Music Review* 22, September 1969.
8 Lewis (not to be confused with Jimmy Lewis on Atlantic, 1949/1950) had been a good soul singer throughout the '60s. *Feelin' In Mah Bones* (4J 508) and *I Have Love (For You)* (4J 512) in 1963 had an organ-based accompaniment and were full of gospel chord changes. He was interviewed by *Soul* in April 1968. 'I started with a friend of mine, James Carmichael. We started out together and he really got me started writing. I was out of school by this time. I wrote a tune, it was my first hit record, I think it was 1963, a thing entitled *Wait Until Spring*. It did very well for me and I went on the road with it. While I was on the road I was working with The Original Drifters. They talked me into joining their group and I sang lead with them for two years. Then I came back and started writing with Jimmy Holiday.' Lewis has recorded

a number of the songs he has written with Holiday, for Minit and Tangerine, during the last three years. One such title, *The Girls From Texas* (Minit 32017), also portrayed an intensely personal church style with Lewis preaching to the listener after the manner of Joe Tex or Solomon Burke. It was a brilliant soul record – a rare commodity in 1968. Patti Drew, Jimmy Holiday and Ray Charles – who has recorded an album of Lewis compositions – have recently recognised his ability as a convincing lyricist.

9 Steve Richards, *Record Mirror*, February 1966.
10 Pinkney's new group contained: Albert Fortson, b. Detroit, 17.6.37, who had sung with Spider and The Astronauts; Benny Anderson, b. Atlanta, 2.9.44, who occasionally took the lead from Pinkney, particularly on high-powered ballads like *Danny Boy*; and Wallace Ezzard, b. 7.6.38. Their guitarist, Mark Williams, b. 27.10.41, came from Alabama and originally led his own group, The Swinging Dukes. Fortson, Anderson and Ezzard sang in Detroit as a trio called The Tears. Before joining Pinkney, they cut two sides for King in 1963. The session, produced by white R&B singer Wayne Cochran (who played bass on both titles), gave rise to *Sugar Girl* and *Little School Girl*. Anderson sang lead.
11 Peter Burns, *Blues and Soul Monthly Music Review*, September/October 1970.
12 Ritchie Yorke, Toronto *Globe and Mail*, 19 December 1968.
13 Charlie Gillett, unpublished interview, 1970.
14 Yorke, op. cit.
15 Jerry Leiber interviewed by Michael March, *Fusion* 39, 21 August 1970.
16 Don Heckman, 'The Fifties', *The Many Worlds of Music*, BMI Publication, 1969.
17 Those who enjoyed British hits by 'covering' The Drifters' material include The Searchers (*Sweets For My Sweet*); Craig Douglas and Jimmy Justice (*When My Little Girl Is Smiling*); Kenny Lynch (*Up On The Roof*); The Moody Blues (*I Don't Want To Go On Without You*); and Cliff Bennett (*One Way Love*). The Rolling Stones' *Under The Boardwalk* sold well abroad. Less successful were The Mudlarks (*True Love, True Love*).

Discography

arr	arranger	hca	harmonica
as	alto saxophone	Lon	London
Atl	Atlantic	orch	orchestra
b	bass	org	organ
bs	baritone saxophone	perc	percussion
cond	conductor	p	piano
d	drums	prod	producer
dir	director	tb	trombone
(E)	British issue	tp	trumpet
f-b	fender bass	ts	tenor saxophone
g	guitar	vo	vocal

'CB' followed by a date, in parentheses after a song-title, refers to the *Cashbox* review of that recording.
Atl 1000/2000s, Lon(E) HLE8000/9000s and HLK9000s, and Atl(E) 4000s are 45 rpm singles; Atl 500/600s, Lon(E) REK1200/1300s, and Atl(E) AET6000s are EPs; all other issues are LPs. The reverse sides of Lon(E) HLE8906, 9000 and 9079 are Clyde McPhatter solos.

CLYDE McPHATTER AND THE DRIFTERS: Clyde McPhatter (lead tenor), Gerhart Thrasher (tenor), Andrew Thrasher (baritone), Willie Ferbee (bass) with Sam 'The Man' Taylor or Ben Webster (ts), p, Mickey Baker (g), b, d. [New York, June 1953]

A-1085	*Gone*	Atl 1055, 8031
A-1086		
A-1087	*Lucille*	Atl 1019, 534, 8024

CLYDE McPHATTER AND THE DRIFTERS: Clyde McPhatter (lead tenor), Gerhart Thrasher (tenor), Andrew Thrasher (baritone), Bill Pinkney (bass) with Sam 'The Man' Taylor (ts), Jesse Stone or Harry Van Walls (p), b, d. [New York, August 1953]

A-1104	*The Way I Feel*	Atl 1006, 534, 8031
A-1105	*Money Honey*	Atl 1006, 534, 8003, 8010, 8077, 8162, Atl(E) 5001, 587 095, 587 144
A-1106		
A-1107		
A-1108	*Let The Boogie Woogie Roll*	Atl 2060

CLYDE McPHATTER AND THE DRIFTERS: same (vo) with Sam 'The Man' Taylor (ts), Harry Van Walls (p), Jimmy Oliver or Mickey Baker (g), b, d. [New York, October 1953]

A-1151	*Don't Dog Me*	Atl 2049, Lon(E) HLE9079
A-1152	*Such A Night*	Atl 1019, 534, 8003, 8077, Atl(E) 5001, 587 144
A-1153	*Warm Your Heart*	Atl 1029, 8003, 8077, Atl(E) 5001, 587 144
A-1154	*Bip Bam* (ts solo)	Atl 1043, 8024

CLYDE McPHATTER AND THE DRIFTERS: same (vo) with possibly Jesse Stone (p), Mickey Baker (g), b, d, vibes—1. McPhatter and Pinkney (vo duet)*. [New York, November 1953]

A-1201	*White Christmas*—1*	Atl 1048, 8003, 8077, Atl(E) 5001, 587 144
A-1202	*The Bells of St Mary* (CB 11.12.54)	Atl 1048, 8003, Atl(E) 587 144
A-1203	*Honey Love*	Atl 1029, 605, 8003, 8010, 8077, 8162, Atl(E) 5001, 587 095, 587 144

| A-1204 | Whatcha Gonna Do | Atl 1055, 605, 8003, 8077, Atl(E) 5001, 587 144 |

CLYDE McPHATTER AND THE DRIFTERS: same (vo) with possibly Maxwell Davis (ts), p, g, b, d. [New York, February 1954]

A-1228	If I Didn't Love You	Atl 2082
A-1229	Someday You'll Want Me To Want You	Atl 1043, 8003, 8077, Atl(E) 5001, 587 144
A-1230	There You Go (ts solo)	Atl 2038, Lon(E) HLE9000
A-1231	Try Try Baby (ts solo)	Atl 2028, 8031, Lon(E) HLE 8906

CLYDE McPHATTER AND VOCAL QUARTET: (vo) with ts, p, g, b, d. [New York, possibly June 1954]

A-1339	Everyone's Laughing (ts solo)	Atl 1070, 8031
A-1340		
A-1341	Hot Ziggety	Atl 1070, 8031

THE DRIFTERS: David Baughn (lead tenor), Gerhart Thrasher (tenor), Andrew Thrasher (baritone), Bill Pinkney (bass/baritone lead—1) with orch, including Sam 'The Man' Taylor, another (ts), p, Mickey Baker or Jimmy Oliver (g), b, Connie Kay (d), Ray Ellis (arr/cond). A Leiber-Stoller Production. [New York, April/May 1955]

A-1510	No Sweet Lovin' (ts solo ST)—1	Atl 2105, 8059, Lon(E) HLK9382, HAK2450
A-1511		
A-1512	Honey Bee (ts solo)	Atl 2096, Lon(E) HLK9326

THE DRIFTERS: Johnny Moore (lead tenor), Gerhart Thrasher (tenor/lead tenor—1), Charlie Hughes (baritone), Bill Pinkney (bass/baritone lead—2) with possibly Buddy Lucas (ts), bs, p, Jimmy Oliver (g), b, d. Supervision: Nesuhi Ertegun. [Hollywood, September 1955]

A-1664	Adorable	Atl 1078, 592, 8022, 8162, Clarion 608, Atl(E) 587 123
A-1665	Your Promise To Be Mine—1	Atl 1089, 8022, Atl(E) 587 123
A-1666	Ruby Baby	Atl 1089, 592, 8022, 8073, 8163, Clarion 608, Atl(E) 588 160, 587 096, 587 123
A-1667	Steamboat—2	Atl 1078, 592, 8022, 8001, Clarion 608, Atl(E) 587 123
A-1668	Drifting Away From You—1	Atl 1141, 8022, Atl(E) 587 123

THE DRIFTERS: same (vo) with ts, p, b, d. [New York, June/July 1956]

A-2046	Soldier of Fortune	Atl 1101, 8022, Lon(E) HLE8344, Atl(E) 587 123
A-2047	Honky Tonky (p solo)	Atl 8041, Lon(E) HAK2318, Atl(E) 590 010
A-2048	I Gotta Get Myself A Woman (ts solo)	Atl 1101, 8022, Lon(E) HLE8344, Atl(E) 587 123
A-2049	Sadie My Lady (ts solo)	Atl 8041, Lon(E) HLK9287, HAK2318, Atl(E) 590 010

THE DRIFTERS: Johnny Moore (lead tenor), Gerhart Thrasher (tenor), Charlie Hughes (baritone), Tommy Evans (bass) with ts, p, Jimmy Oliver (g), b, d. Supervision: Ahmet Ertegun and Jerry Wexler. [New York, November 1956]

| A-2184 | It Was A Tear | Atl 1123, 8022, Atl(E) 587 123 |
| A-2185 | Fools Fall In Love | Atl 1123, 592, 8163, Clarion 608, Atl(E) 587 123 |

THE DRIFTERS: same (vo) with ts, bs, p, Jimmy Oliver (g), b, d. Supervision: Ahmet Ertegun and Jerry Wexler. [New York, March 1957]

A-2374	Yodee Yakee (ts solo)	Atl 1161, 8022, Atl(E) 587 123
A-2375	Souvenirs	Atl 8041, Lon(E) HAK2318, Atl(E) 590 010
A-2376	Hypnotized (ts solo)	Atl 1141, 8022, Atl(E) 587 123
A-2377	I Know	Atl 1161, 8022, Atl(E) 587 123

THE DRIFTERS: Bobby Hendricks (lead tenor), Gerhart Thrasher (tenor), Charlie Hughes (baritone), Bill Pinkney (bass) with the Ray Ellis Orchestra, including as, ts, p, Jimmy Oliver (g), b, d. Hendricks and Pinkney (vo duet)*. The Ray Ellis Singers replace The Drifters—1. Supervision: Ahmet Ertegun and Jerry Wexler. [New York, 1958]

A-3051	Drip Drop (ts solo)	Atl 1187, 8022, 8093, Clarion 608, Lon(E) HLE8686, Atl(E) 5015, 587 123, 587 038
A-3052	Suddenly There's A Valley*	Atl 2087, 8041, Lon(E) HAK2318, Atl(E) 590 010
A-3053	Moonlight Bay (as, ts)—1	Atl 1187, 8022, 8037, Lon(E) HLE8686, HAE2180, Atl(E) 587 123

THE FIVE CROWNS: James 'Poppa' Clark, Wilber 'Younky' Paul, Claud 'Little Nickie' Clark, John 'Big John' Clark and Dock 'Doc' Green (vo group). [New York, 1952]

4000	You're My Inspiration	Rainbow 179	
4001	A Star	—	
4009	$19.50 Bus	Rainbow 184	
4010	Who Can Be True	—	
4060	Why Don't You Believe Me	Rainbow 202	
4062	Keep It A Secret	—	
4063	Alone Again	Rainbow 206	[1953]
4064	I Don't Have To Hurt No More	—	
	I Was Wrong	Rainbow 281	[1953]
	Hug Me Baby	—	
770	Good Luck Darlin'	Old Town 790	[1952]
771	You Could Be My Love	—	

795	*Lullabye Of The Bells*	Old Town 792	[1952–3]
796	*Later Later Baby*	—	
			[1955]
RIV-6132	*Ooo-Wee Baby*	Riviera 990, Rainbow 335	
		(as THE DUVALS)	
RIV-6133	*You Came To Me*	—	
RR 3029	*Do You Remember*	Gee 1001	[1956]
RR 3030	*God Bless You*	—	

Ben E King (lead), Charles Thomas (tenor), Doc Green (baritone), Ellsbury Hobbs (bass).
[New York, 1958]

A	*Kiss And Make Up*	R & B 6901 (as THE CROWNS)
B	*I'll Forget About You*	—
		[? 1958]
TW-717 A	*Popcorn Willy*	Trans-World 717, Caravan 15609
TW-717 B	*I Can't Pretend*	—

THE DRIFTERS (formerly The Crowns): Ben E King (lead baritone), Charles Thomas (tenor), Doc Green (baritone), Ellsbury Hobbs (bass) with King Curtis (ts), p, Reggie Kimber (g), b, d, bells—1, strings—2. A Leiber-Stoller Production. [New York, March 1959]

A-3396	*Hey Senorita* (ts solo)	Atl 2062, 8041, Lon(E) HAK2318, HLK9145, Atl(E) 590 010
A-3397	*There Goes My Baby*—2	Atl 2025, 8037, 8041, 8073, 8153, 8164, Clarion 608, Lon(E) HLE8892, HAK2318, Atl(E) 590 010, 588 160, 587 103, 587 097, 587 109
A-3398	*Baltimore* (ts solo)	Atl 2050, 8041, Lon(E) HLE9081, HAK2318, 590 010
A-3399	*Oh My Love*—1	Atl 2025, 8041, Lon(E) HLE8892, HAK2318, 590 010

THE DRIFTERS: Ben E King (lead baritone), Johnny Lee Williams (lead tenor—1), Charles Thomas (tenor), Doc Green (baritone), Ellsbury Hobbs (bass) with strings, p—2, Billy Davis (g), b, d, bells.
[New York, August 1959]

| A-3726 | *True Love True Love*—1 | Atl 2040, 8041, 8073, 8153, 8164, Lon(E) HLE8988, HAK2318, Atl(E) 590 010, 588 160, 587 103, 587 097 |
| A-3727 | *Dance With Me*—2 | Atl 2040, 8041, 8164, 8153, Lon(E) HLE8988, HAK2318, HA 8131, REK1282, Atl(E) 590 010, 587 061, 587 097, 587 109 |

THE DRIFTERS: Ben E King (lead baritone), Charles Thomas (tenor), Doc Green (baritone), Ellsbury Hobbs (bass) with strings, bs, p, Billy Davis (g), b, d. [New York, December 1959]

| A-3987 | *This Magic Moment* | Atl 2050, 8041, 8073, 8153, 8164, Lon(E) HLE9081, HAK2318, REK1282, Atl(E) 590 010, 588 160, 587 103, 587 097 |
| A-3988 | *Lonely Winds* | Atl 2062, 8041, Clarion 608, Lon(E) HLK9145, HAK2318, Atl(E) 590 010 |

THE DRIFTERS: same (vo) with strings, p, Billy Davis (g), b, d, choir—1, Stan Applebaum (arr/dir).
A Leiber-Stoller Production. [New York, May 1960]

A-4565	*Save The Last Dance For Me*—1	Atl 2071, 8059, 8073, 8153, 8164, Clarion 608, Mercury LP20809, Lon(E) HA8129, HAK2450, REK1282, HLK 9201, Atl(E) 5020, 584 090, 588 160, 587 103, 587 907
A-4566	*Nobody But Me*	Atl 2071, 8059, Lon(E) HLK9201, HAK2450
A-4567	*I Count The Tears*	Atl 2087, 8059, 8153, 8164, Lon(E) HLK9287, HAK2450, REK1282, Atl(E) 587 103, 587 097
A-4568	*Sometimes I Wonder*	Atl 2151, Lon(E) REK1282

THE DRIFTERS: Rudy Lewis (lead), Charles Thomas (tenor), Doc Green (baritone), Ellsbury Hobbs (bass) with Dionne and Dee Dee Warwick, Cissy Houston, Doris Troy (vo), Mort Shuman (p), Billy Davis (g), b, d, bongos, strings, Burt Bacharach (arr). A Leiber-Stoller Production.
[New York, September 1960]

A-5323	*Room Full of Tears*	Atl 2127, 8059, 8073, Lon(E) HLK9500, HAK2450, Atl(E) 588 160
A-5324	*Please Stay*	Atl 2105, 8059, Lon(E) HLK9382, HAK2450
A-5325	*Sweets For My Sweet*	Atl 2117, 8059, 8073, Lon(E) HLK9427, HAK2450, HA8148, REK1390, Atl(E) 5020, 588 160
A-5326	*Some Kind of Wonderful*	Atl 2096, 8059, Clarion 608, Lon(E) HLK9326, HAK2450

THE DRIFTERS: Rudy Lewis (lead), Charles Thomas (tenor), Doc Green (baritone), Tommy Evans (bass), with Dionne and Dee Dee Warwick, Cissy Houston, Doris Troy (vo), strings, p, Billy Davis (g), b, d, Burt Bacharach (arr). A Leiber-Stoller Production. [New York, July 1961]

A-5630	*Loneliness Or Happiness*	Atl 2117, 8073, Lon(E) HLK9427, Atl(E) 588 160
A-5631	*Mexican Divorce*	Atl 2134, 8059, 8073, Lon(E) HLK9522, HAK2450, Atl(E) 588 160
A-5632	*Somebody New Dancing With You*	Atl 2127, 8059, Clarion 608, Lon(E) HLK9500, HAK2450

THE DRIFTERS: same (vo) with same female quartet (vo), p, Billy Davis, another (g), b, d, timbales. A Leiber-Stoller Production. [New York, December 1961]

A-5743	*Jackpot*	Atl 2151, 8059, Lon(E) HAK2450, REK1355
A-5744	*When My Little Girl is Smiling*	Atl 2134, 8059, 8073, Lon(E) HLK9522, HAK2450, HA8171, REK1355, Atl(E) 588 160

THE DRIFTERS: same (vo) with orch including strings, hca, p, Billy Davis (g), b, d, Klaus Ogermann (arr/cond). [New York, May 1962]

A-6031	*Stranger On The Shore* (hca solo)	Atl 2143, 8073, Lon(E) HLK9554, Atl(E) 588 160
A-6032	*What To Do* (hca solo)	Atl 2143, 8073, Lon(E) HLK9554, Atl(E) 588 160

THE DRIFTERS: Rudy Lewis (lead), Charles Thomas (tenor), Eugene Pearson (baritone), Tommy Evans (bass) with orch, Bert Keyes (arr/dir). Same female quartet (vo). A Leiber-Stoller Production. [New York, November 1962]

A-6356	*Another Night With The Boys*	Atl 2162, 8073, Lon(E) HLK9626, Atl(E) 588 160
A-6357	*Up On The Roof* (CB 29.9.62)	Atl 2162, 8073, 8093, 8099, 8153, Lon(E) HLK9626, HA8213, REK1355, Atl(E) 5015, 587 038, 588 103
A-6358	*I Feel Good All Over*	Atl 2201, 8093, 8099, Lon(E) HLK9785, Atl(E) 5015, 587 038

THE DRIFTERS: same (vo) with same female quartet (vo) and unknown personnel. [New York, January 1963]

A-6743	*Let The Music Play*	Atl 2182, 8073, 8099, Lon(E) HLK9699, REK1385, Atl(E) 5015, 587 038
A-6744	*On Broadway* (CB 9.3.63)	Atl 2182, 8093, 8099, 8153, 8194, Lon(E) HLK9699, REK1385, Atl(E) 5015, 587 038, 588 103, 587 141

THE DRIFTERS: Rudy Lewis (lead), Johnny Moore (lead tenor—1), Charles Thomas (tenor), Eugene Pearson (baritone), Tommy Evans or Johnny Terry (bass) with orch, Garry Sherman (arr/dir). [New York, April 1963]

A-6918		
A-6920	*Rat Race* (CB 1.6.63)	Atl 2191, 8093, 8099, Lon(E) HLK9750, REK1385, Atl(E) 5015, 587 038
A-6921	*If You Don't Come Back*—1	Atl 2191, 8093, 8099, Lon(E) HLK9750, REK1385, Atl(E) 5015, 587 038
A-6922	*I'll Take You Home*—1	Atl 2201, 8093, 8099, Lon(E) HLK9785, Atl(E) 5015, 587 038
A-6932		

THE DRIFTERS: Rudy Lewis (lead), Johnny Moore (lead tenor—1), Charles Thomas (tenor), Eugene Pearson (baritone), Johnny Terry (bass) with Billy Davis (g), b, d, org, strings, same female quartet (vo), Garry Sherman (arr/cond). Produced by Bert Berns. [New York, August 1963]

A-7172	*In The Land Of Make Believe*	Atl 2216, 8093, 8099, Lon(E) HLK9848, Atl(E) 5015, 587 038
A-7173	*Didn't It* (org solo)—1	Atl 2225, 8093, 8099, Lon(E) HLK9886, Atl(E) 5015, 587 038

THE DRIFTERS: same (vo) and same female quartet (vo) and unknown personnel. [New York, December 1963]

A-7467	*One Way Love*—1	Atl 2225, 8093, 8099, Lon(E) HLK9886, Atl(E) 5015, 587 038
A-7468	*Vaya Con Dios*	Atl 2216, 8093, 8099, Lon(E) HLK9848, Atl(E) 5015, 587 038

THE DRIFTERS: Johnny Moore (lead), Charles Thomas (lead baritone—1), Eugene Pearson (baritone), Johnny Terry (bass) with orch, Teacho Wilshire (arr/cond). Produced by Bert Berns. [New York, May 1964]

A-7922	*Under The Boardwalk*	Atl 2237, 8099, Atl(E) 4001, 587 038, AET6003

A-7923		
A-7924	*He's Just A Playboy*	Atl 2253, 8113, Atl(E) 4008, 5039, 587 061, AET6003
A-7925	*I Don't Want To Go On Without You*—1	Atl 2237, 8113, Atl(E) 4001, 5039, 587 061, AET6003

THE DRIFTERS: same (vo) with strings, 2 tp, p, Billy Davis, another (g), b, d, Teacho Wilshire (arr/dir). Produced by Bert Berns. [New York, 1964]

A-8057	*I've Got Sand In My Shoes*	Atl 2253, 8113, 8153, Atl(E) 4008, 5039, AET6003, 587 061, 588 103
A-8058	*Saturday Night At The Movies*	Atl 2260, 8153, Atl(E) 4012

THE DRIFTERS: same (vo) and unknown personnel. Produced by Bert Berns. [New York, 1964]

A-8234	*Spanish Lace* (CB 9.11.64)	Atl 2260, 8113, Atl(E) 4012, 5039, 587 061

THE DRIFTERS: same (vo) with orch, Richard Wess (arr/cond)—1, Ray Ellis (arr/cond)—2. Produced by Bert Berns, Tom Dowd. [New York, 1964]

A-8265	*The Christmas Song*—1	Atl 2261
A-8266	*I Remember Christmas*—1	Atl 2261
A-8267		
A-8268		
A-8269	*As Long As She Needs Me*—2	Atl 8103, Atl(E) 5023
A-8270		
A-8271	*The Good Life*—2	Atl 8103, Atl(E) 5023

THE DRIFTERS: same (vo) with orch, Ray Ellis (arr/cond). Produced by Bert Berns, Tom Dowd. [New York, 1964]

A-8276	*Quando Quando Quando*	Atl 8103, Atl(E) 5023
A-8277	*Desafinado*	Atl 8103, Atl(E) 5023

THE DRIFTERS: same (vo) with orch, strings, 2 tp, p, Billy Davis, another (g), b, d, Teacho Wilshire (arr/dir). [New York, 1964]

A-8324	*At The Club*	Atl 2268, 8113, Atl(E) 4019, 5039, 587 061

THE DRIFTERS: same (vo) with orch, Ray Ellis (arr/cond). Produced by Bert Berns, Tom Dowd. [New York, 1964]

A-8341	*I Wish You Love*	Atl 8103, Atl(E) 5023
A-8342	*Tonight*	— —
A-8343	*More*	— —
A-8344	*What Kind Of Fool Am I*	— —

THE DRIFTERS: same (vo) with orch, Ray Ellis or Stanley Applebaum (—1) (arr/cond). Produced by Bert Berns, Tom Dowd. [New York, 1964]

A-8348	*Who Can I Turn To*	Atl 8103, Atl(E) 5023
A-8349		
A-8350	*Temptation*—1	Atl 8103, Atl(E) 5023
A-8351	*On The Street Where You Live*	— —

THE DRIFTERS: same (vo) on 'Live from The Brooklyn Fox in his Record-Breaking Show – Murray The K'. [New York, 1964]

Unknown title(s)   KFM 1001

THE DRIFTERS: same (vo), with Charles Thomas (lead—1) on 'Saturday Night at The Uptown' with orch including Billy Davis (g). Produced by Jerry Wexler, Tom Dowd.
[Uptown Theater, Philadelphia, Pa., 1964]

	Under The Boardwalk (g solo)	Atl 8101, Atl(E) 5018, 588 122
	On Broadway (g solo)	— — —
	There Goes My Baby—1	— — —

THE DRIFTERS: same (vo) with orch, including strings, p, Billy Davis, another (g), b, d, Teacho Wilshire (arr/dir). [New York, 1964]

A-8447	*Answer The Phone* (g solo)	Atl 2268, 8113, Atl(E) 4019, 5039, 587 061

THE DRIFTERS: same (vo) on 'Murray The K's Greatest Holiday Show live from The Brooklyn Fox' with Earl Warren Orchestra, 2 tp, ts, bs, trombones, org, Billy Davis (g), b, d. Engineers: Tom Dowd and Joe Atkinson. [New York, January 1965]

	Under The Boardwalk	Brook-lyn 301, Atl(E) 5026
	Saturday Night At The Movies	— —

THE DRIFTERS: same (vo). [New York, 1965]

A-8670	*Saturday Night At The Movies*	Atl 8103, Atl(E) 5023

THE DRIFTERS: same (vo) with Charles Thomas (lead—1) and orch, Bert Keyes (arr/dir).
[New York, 1965]

A-8746	*Follow Me*	Atl 2292, 8113, Atl(E) 4034, 5039, 587 061
A-8747	*Chains Of Love*—1	Atl 2285, 8113, Atl(E) 4023, 5039, 587 061
A-8748	*Far From The Maddening Crowd*	Atl 2298, 8113, Atl(E) 4040, 5039, 587 061
A-8749	*Come On Over To My Place*	Atl 2285, 8113, Atl(E) 4023, 5039, 587 061

THE DRIFTERS: same (vo) with orch, Charles Thomas (lead—1). [New York, June 1965]

A-8940	*The Outside World*—1	Atl 2292, 8113, Atl(E) 4034, 5039, 587 061
A-8941		
A-8942		
A-8943		

THE DRIFTERS: same (vo) with orch, Gene Page (arr/dir). Produced by Bert Berns.
[New York, 1965]

A-9077

A-9078	I'll Take You Where The Music's Playing	Atl 2298, 8113, Atl(E) 4040, 584 152, 5039, 587 061, 588 027
A-9079	Nylon Stockings	Atl 2310, Atl(E) 4062
A-9080	We Gotta Sing	Atl 2310, Atl(E) 4062

THE DRIFTERS: same (vo) with Charles Thomas (lead—1) and orch, trumpets, trombones, ts, bs, p, g, b, d, per, Artie Butler (arr/dir). Produced by Bert Berns. [New York, February 1966]

A-9800	Up In The Streets of Harlem	Atl 2336, Atl(E) 584 020
A-9881	Memories Are Made Of This	Atl 2325, Atl(E) 4084
A-9882	You Can't Love Them All—1	Atl 2336, Atl(E) 584 020

THE DRIFTERS: same (vo). [New York, 1966]

A-9912	My Islands In The Sun	Atl 2325, Atl(E) 4084

THE DRIFTERS: Johnny Moore (lead), Charles Thomas (tenor), Gene Pearson or Rick Sheppard (baritone), William Brent or Dan Dandridge (bass) with orch, trumpets, tb, ts, bs, Billy Dav (g), f-b, d, Bert Keyes (arr/dir). Produced by Bert Berns. [New York, 1966]

A-10545	Aretha	Atl 2366, Atl(E) 584 090

THE DRIFTERS: same (vo) with orch, strings, trumpets, trombones, ts, bs, p, Billy Davis (g), f-b, d, Bob Gallo (arr/dir). Produced by Bob Gallo and Tom Dowd. [New York, 1966]

A-11081	Baby What I Mean	Atl 2366, Atl(E) 584 090

THE DRIFTERS: Johnny Moore (lead), Bill Fredericks (baritone lead—1), Rick Sheppard (tenor), Charles Thomas (bass) with orch, trumpets, trombones, ts, bs, p, org, Billy Davis (g), f-b, d, conga, Ronnie Savoy (prod). [New York, 1967]

A-12371	Ain't It The Truth—1	Atl 2426
A-12372		
A-12373	Up Jumped The Devil—1	Atl 2426

THE DRIFTERS: same (vo) with orch, Robert Bateman, Lou Courtney (arr). [New York, 1967]

A-13454	Still Burning In My Heart	Atl 2471, Atl(E) 584 195
A-13455	I Need You Now—1	Atl 2471, Atl(E) 584 195

THE DRIFTERS: Johnny Moore (lead), Bill Fredericks (baritone—1), Butch Leake (baritone), Charles Thomas or Milton Turner or Don Thomas (bass) with orch, Jerry Williams Jnr, Garry Sherman (prod/arr). [New York, 1969]

A-16507	Your Best Friend	Atl 2624
A-16508	Steal Away—1	Atl 2624

THE DRIFTERS: Bill Fredericks (lead), Johnny Moore (tenor), Butch Leake (baritone), Don Thomas (bass) with orch including Ben Westerfield (g), Rupert Holmes (arr/cond). Produced by Paul Vance. [New York, 1970]

A-19179	Black Silk	Atl 2746
A-19180	You Got To Pay Your Dues	Atl 2746

Appendix 1: The Drifters' Lead Singers

The Drifters' lead singers and, expressed as a percentage, their contribution to the groups' work (issued recordings only)

Vocalist	Per cent as lead	Period with Drifters		
JOHNNY MOORE	42.7	1955	—	Present
CLYDE McPHATTER	15.3	1953	—	1954
RUDY LEWIS	14.5	1960	—	1963
BEN E KING	8.9	1959	—	1960
BILL FREDERICKS	4.9	1966	—	Present
CHARLES THOMAS	4.03	1959	—	1969
BILL PINKNEY	3.23	1953	—	1958
BOBBY HENDRICKS	1.6		1958	
GERHART THRASHER	1.6	1953	—	1958
DAVID BAUGHN	.8		1955	
CHARLIE HUGHES	.8	1955	—	1958
JOHNNY LEE WILLIAMS	.8		1959	

Appendix 2: The Drifters' Hit Records 1953-70

Year	Groups who entered the R&B Top Ten (numerals in parentheses indicate the number of hits)	Drifters' records with number of release	Dated position reached in national Top '100' Records	Dated position reached in R&B Top 10 Chart
1953	Five Royales (4), Dominoes (4), Clovers (2), Spaniels, Royals, Vocaleers, Four Tunes	Money Honey	(1006)	1 1.11.53
1954	Midnighters (4), Clovers (4), Spiders (2), Counts, Four Tunes, Penguins, Chords, Crows, Spaniels, Moonglows, Charms	Lucille Such A Night Honey Love Bip Bam	(1019) (1019) (1029) (1043)	7 3-4-54 5 3-4-54 1 October 1954 1954*
1955	Five Keys (2), Platters (2), Charms (2), Four Fellows, Jacks, Nutmegs, Spiders, Eldorados, Midnighters, Cardinals, Hearts	White Christmas Whatcha Gonna Do	(1048) (1055)	80 14.12.55 96 25.12.60 88 22.12.62	3 1.1.55 8 4.6.55
1956	Teenagers (5), Platters (3), Clovers (3), Coasters, Cadets, Six Teens, Dells, Cadillacs, Cleftones, Teen Queens, Flamingos, Five Satins, Charms, Jayhawks, Heartbeats	Adorable Steamboat Ruby Baby Soldier Of Fortune I Gotta Get Myself A Woman	(1078) (1078) (1089) (1101) (1101)		January 1956* 9 7.1.56 1956* 1956*
1957	Coasters (2), Del-Vikings (2), Rays (2), Tuneweavers, Danny and The Juniors, Diamonds, Five Royales, Charms, Five Satins, Bobbettes, Dominoes	Fools Fall In Love Hypnotised	(1123) (1141)	69 March 1957 79 29.6.57	
1958	Platters (2), Silhouettes, Diamonds, Monotones, Quintones, Impressions, Crescendoes, Elegants, Moonglows, Chantels, Imperials, Royal Teens, Teddy Bears	Moonlight Bay Drip Drop	(1187) (1187)	72 June 1958 58 24.8.58	
1959	Coasters (2), Fleetwoods (2), Spacemen, Platters, Flamingos, Skyliners, Crests, Fiestas, Falcons, Midnighters	There Goes My Baby Dance With Me True Love, True Love	(2025) (2040) (2040)	2 18.8.59 15 1.12.59 33 October 1959	3 3.8.59 2 16.11.59 10 28.12.59
1960	Midnighters (3), Hollywood Argyles, Olympics, Zodiacs, Miracles	This Magic Moment Lonely Winds Save The Last Dance For Me	(2050) (2062) (2071)	16 29.3.60 54 June 1960 1 18.10.60	4 4.4.60 9 27.6.60 1 31.10.60

Year	Groups who entered the R&B Top Ten (numerals in parentheses indicate the number of hits)	Drifters' records with number of release		Dated position reached in national Top '100' Records	Dated position reached in R&B Top 10 Chart	
1961	Midnighters (4), Shirelles (3), Rosie and The Originals, Cleftones, Regents, Jarmels, Marcels, Chantels, Dovells, Jive Five, Chanters, Limelites, Pips, Marvelettes, Impressions, Simms Twins, Crystals, Spinners	I Count The Tears Some Kind Of Wonderful Please Stay Sweets For My Sweet Room Full Of Tears	(2087) (2096) (2105) (2117) (2127)	17 32 14 16 72	31.1.61 13.5.61 25.7.61 29.10.61 December 1961	9 10	13.2.61 May 1961* 22.10.61
1962	Marvelettes (3), Shirelles (2), Four Seasons (2), Orlons (2), Contours, Pips, Crystals, Falcons, Ikettes, Tokens, Sensations, Valentinos, Limelites, Corsairs, Exciters, Isley Brothers	When My Little Girl Is Smiling Stranger On The Shore	(2134) (2143)	28 73	7.4.62 12.5.62		
1963	Cookies (2), Martha and The Vandellas (2), Crystals (2), Chiffons (2), Orlons (2), Miracles (2), Ronettes, Essex, Shirelles, Impressions, Marvelettes, Dovells, Angels, Cascades, Ruby and The Romantics, Jaynetts, Tymes, Four Seasons, Bob B Soxx and The Blue Jeans	Up On The Roof On Broadway Rat Race If You Don't Come Back I'll Take You Home	(2162) (2182) (2191) (2191) (2201)	5 9 71 101 25	9.2.63 27.4.63 6.7.63 20.7.63 19.10.63	4 7 24	9.2.63 4.5.63 12.10.63
1964		Vaya Con Dios One Way Love Under The Boardwalk Sand In My Shoes He's Just A Playboy Saturday Night At The Movies	(2216) (2225) (2237) (2253) (2253) (2260)	43 56 4 33 115 18	29.2.64 6.6.64 22.8.64 24.10.64 7.11.64 19.12.64	Billboard did not publish an R&B chart between 30.11.63 and 23.1.65	
1965	Supremes (5), Four Tops (4), Temptations (4), Miracles (3), Impressions (2), Adlibs, Marvelows, Anthony and The Imperials, Spinners, Larks, Toys	At The Club Chains Of Love Come On Over To My Place Follow Me I'll Take You Where The Music's Playing	(2268) (2285) (2285) (2292) (2298)	43 90 60 91 51	13.2.65 24.4.65 22.5.65 17.7.65 18.9.65	10	13.2.65
1966	Supremes (4), Temptations (3), Four Tops (2), Martha and The Vandellas (2), Elgins (2), Capitols, Poets, Vontastics, Marvelettes, Platters, Mad Lads, Artistics, COD's, Holidays, Isley Brothers	Nylon Stockings Memories Are Made Of This Up In The Streets Of Harlem Baby What I Mean	(2310) (2325) (2336) (2366)	48 62	23.4.66 December 1966	37	24.12.66
1967		Ain't It The Truth	(2436)				
1968		Still Burning In My Heart	(2471)	111	20.1.68		
1969		Steal Away	(2624)				
1970		You Gotta Pay Your Dues	(2746)				

PUBLIC LIBRARY
DISTRICT OF COLUMBIA

BLACK STUDIES
REFERENCE ONLY

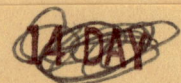

BL. ST.

**PROPERTY OF THE
DISTRICT OF COLUMBIA**

Theft or mutilation
is punishable by law

P.L. 117